JUST
KEEP
CLIMBING

JUST
KEEP
CLIMBING

INSPIRATIONAL STORIES
FOR OVERCOMING CHALLENGES
AND LIVING LIFE

BARRY FINLAY

OTHER BOOKS BY BARRY FINLAY

NON-FICTION

Kilimanjaro and Beyond: A Life-Changing Journey
I Guess We Missed the Boat

FICTION

THE MARCIE KANE THRILLER COLLECTION
The Vanishing Wife
A Perilous Question
Remote Access
Never So Alone
The Burden of Darkness

THE JAKE SCOTT MYSTERY SERIES
Searching For Truth
The Guardians of Truth

DEDICATED TO
ANYONE
FACING
CHALLENGES,
BIG OR SMALL.

Published by Keep On Climbing Publishing

© Barry Finlay 2023

(613) 240-6953
info@barry-finlay.com
www.barry-finlay.com

Cataloguing data available at Library and Archives Canada.
ISBN: 978-1-7771395-9-9

CONTENTS

ACKNOWLEDGEMENTS

J*ust Keep Climbing* is a milestone for me as it represents my tenth published book. As usual, it takes a team to pull it together, but this one is special. Not only is there the usual cast of designers, formatters, advance readers, and family who helped bring the book to fruition, there are several special people who contributed their inspirational stories, and I can't thank them enough.

Each was tremendous to work with and responded to my questions patiently and quickly, even though they have their own deadlines, family responsibilities, and other daily occurrences. If you are inspired by *Just Keep Climbing*, join me in thanking Jen Gilroy, Gabriella Varga and her daughters, Paige and Kiera, Karla Del Grande, Karen Meades, Dan Crépault, Brian Singh, Elisa Magagna, and Edwin (no last name for reasons you will discover later). My life is richer for having been introduced to these people, and I think you will agree that yours will be, too.

Several people suggested I write this book, but probably no one advocated more strongly for it than Erin Quinn, and I'm grateful for that. The hundreds of people who have quoted my motto, "Every mountain top is within reach if you just keep climbing," on social media provided further impetus. I haven't met any of them personally, but they unwittingly encouraged me to write my own story and to include the stories of others.

Thank you to my advance readers who offered insight and suggestions for improvement. I find I get too close to a book as I'm writing and having extra eyes on it before it's finalized is invaluable.

I also deeply appreciate the readers who keep me writing. A special shout out to the fans of my thrillers and mysteries who are patiently waiting. The next Jake Scott mystery is coming, I promise.

I want to thank the people who put the "nuts and bolts" of the book together. Thank you to Katie Baker, who did an amazing and thorough job of editing the manuscript. I'm very proud of the cover and have David Provolo to thank for that. The formatting was completed by Megan Sheer, and I'm very grateful for her work.

Finally, I would like to thank my family. Sons, Trevor and Christopher, provided their input to the book, for which I'm deeply appreciative. My wife, Evelyn, is always the first to read the unedited, unpolished manuscript and provides valuable suggestions. This book is about people who create their own challenges or who have challenges they didn't ask for. Evelyn deals with physical issues daily with strength, determination, and good humor. As she says, "It's okay to be in pain, but you don't have to be one." Her love and support are boundless, and she epitomizes the strength and determination required to Just Keep Climbing.

INTRODUCTION

CHAPTER ONE

JUST KEEP CLIMBING

January 16, 2009. For most, it was probably a day like any other. Even the internet had little to say that day, which is unusual. People talked about the ditching of US Airways Flight 1549 in the Hudson River, but that happened the day before. For me, January 16, 2009 was a day I'll always remember.

I got up that morning after having spent six days on the side of Africa's highest mountain, Mount Kilimanjaro. Our son, Chris, and I slept fitfully on the cold mountainside during the night. Pretty much everything ached, and the limited air made tying our shoelaces a struggle. Put your hand over your nose and mouth as you read this, and you'll have an idea of what I'm talking about. We suffered varying degrees of altitude sickness as we faced a steep incline on loose rock in a whistling cold wind, battling fatigue, and, in Chris's case, injury, with limited air to breathe.

We could hardly wait to get started.

The word "adversity" comes to mind, but only because it's so often overused, especially by the sports community. Did we face adversity? I prefer to say we faced a challenge and save the word "adversity" for bigger things you'll read about later. The day would be the culmination of everything we worked for over a year to achieve. The day would change my life.

It was summit day.

I have spent countless hours reliving the adventure and making presentations about the climb and everything that went into it. I've thought long and hard about the changes in my life brought about by the adventure, and it made me reconsider everything leading up to that day on the mountain. With our fatigued legs, we slipped and slid on the shale, scrambled over and around craggy boulders, and wandered through lush rainforests and barren landscapes. As we neared the end of a long day of hiking, a voice from the back of the pack urged us to "keep swimming." It was Chris reminding us that the way to the top was by persevering. It seemed so appropriate and spurred us on. We chuckled at the time as we peered through the fog and clouds in the seemingly endless distance to glimpse the flag where our next campsite should be. Two to three years later, I realized we did as Chris suggested. We weren't swimming, of course, but we just kept climbing. Then it occurred to me that climbing that mountain, or any hill, is a metaphor for life. We face all kinds of challenges in our lives that can seem like mountains, whether large or small. *Every mountain top is within reach if you just keep climbing* became my mantra.

The only way to overcome challenges (reach the top of our mountain) is to keep going. Nobody's path is a straight line throughout their lives. There are hills and mountains to climb. Our mountains could be any size, but they might seem like Mount Everest to us when we're going over or, sometimes, through them.

EVERY MOUNTAIN TOP IS WITHIN REACH IF YOU JUST KEEP CLIMBING.

They arise from an early age and stand in our way throughout our lives. From the time we start kindergarten, the challenge might be to find and keep friends. We're expected to decide what to do with our lives when we near graduation. As we get older, the challenges start to pile up: job search, marriage, raising kids, aging parents, medical issues... The challenges never end, but the only way we can overcome them is to put one foot in front of the other and keep climbing.

When we decided to climb the mountain, I resolved to do everything I could to prepare for the climb, and whatever would be would be. Altitude sickness, fatigue, or some kind of injury, like a twisted ankle, might prevent me from making it to the top. My definition of success changed as I prepared for and started the climb, but my overall measure would be that I had given it my best shot. I didn't want to leave anything on that mountainside. Even if I didn't complete the climb, with enough training, I would be physically capable. If I still didn't reach the top, it would be disappointing, but it could be considered a success.

There is no question we were privileged to be on that mountain that day. Nobody forced us to be there. It was a challenge we gave ourselves, and we found the financial means to go. Yes, I'm privileged, but I also believe privilege is gained partly through luck. I consider myself lucky to be born in Canada to parents who raised my three brothers and me with values and a strong work ethic. I consider myself lucky to have been raised on a farm near a small town. Some might argue that the late forties and early fifties turned out to be the right time to be born. But in my mind, privilege also comes from the choices we make, dedication, perseverance, taking chances, making mistakes, and a lot of hard work.

The preparation for the climb and reaching the summit changed my life, and I'll try to summarize it. It made me realize that with dedication and hard work, we can reach our goals, or at least make our best attempt to do so. My lifestyle changed because of climbing that mountain. I continue to eat well and try to make exercise part of my weekly routine. We used the mountain as a platform to raise money for the children of Tanzania and, over time, raised enough funds to complete four projects in that country and provide donations to the Wounded Warriors Canada service dog program, as well. That experience taught me that a person can not only change their own life, but with a little effort, we can also change the lives of others. The travel to Africa solidified my understanding that people are people everywhere. We all hope and dream. Because of circumstances beyond our control, we may not all have the same opportunities to reach the top of our mountain, but we all have it in us to try.

Sometimes, we need to look around for a little inspiration to give us the boost to dig a little deeper. Throughout this book, I'll reflect on the lessons learned through my experiences and those of eight others. I was sixty when I climbed the mountain in 2009. Now, I'm on the downward slope of life, but I've enjoyed every minute. I've never stopped learning, and to learn, we must watch, listen, take risks, make our mistakes,

and try again. Aging brings with it many positives, and one of the greatest is the benefit of looking in the rear-view mirror.

Life is backwards in a way. Later in the book, you will meet Edwin, who brought an African proverb to my attention, "What an elder sees while sitting, a younger man cannot see even if he climbs a tree." We gain the wisdom we could have used in our youth as we progress through life. But the young have the option of listening to and learning from their elders while making their own mistakes. I hope this book will help with that process. I also hope, in a way, it will give our youth something to look forward to as we examine how age isn't a barrier to fulfilling our hopes and dreams.

Two people gave me the same advice when I was considering climbing a mountain at sixty years of age. One was my brother, Keith, who was seriously ill in a hospital bed when Chris and I left for Tanzania. The other was my wife, Evelyn, who was going to stay home to write the blog while we tested ourselves on Mount Kilimanjaro. Both said, "If it's something you want to do, do it."

I'm not a philosopher or a psychologist. I'm an accountant who turned to writing in my retirement years. I've had a great life with a wonderful family who supported me each time I took on a new challenge. Whatever the challenge is, big or small, I see inspiration to just keep climbing everywhere. It might be someone who has successfully taken on a life-changing journey, like our climb, or someone who has taken a risk to pursue their passion. It could be someone working their butt off to prepare for a challenge, who hasn't quite reached their goal yet. Maybe it's someone who has been to a personal hell and fought their way back. It could be the indomitable spirit of someone who is still in hell but putting one foot in front of the other just to keep going. They are all inspirational, and you'll read examples of each one.

Eight people shared their stories with me for this book, and I'll be forever grateful. They all had their reasons for facing their challenge, and their stories inspired me. I suspect not one of them realizes how inspiring their stories are. Some took a risk to chase a dream and caught it. Others overcame tremendous odds to defeat personal demons. Their challenges all came about by choice. They all had offramps to take, should things go wrong. One is courageously battling cancer, while another is in the middle of a conflict in his country. The latter two have no offramps; no choice but to face their challenges, and they're doing it heroically. Each of these people is putting one foot in front of the other to meet their respective challenges. The stories are personal, emotional, raw, and uplifting.

Common themes are central to each of the stories. They are stories about ordinary people doing extraordinary things. We can't compare ourselves to any of them, but we can use their stories for inspiration and apply them to our own challenges. Each defines success differently, and you'll read how each satisfies themselves that they either reached their peak or are doing everything they can under difficult circumstances to make it to the top.

They all just keep climbing.

CHAPTER TWO

WHY THIS BOOK AND WHY NOW?

I think we can all agree, there's a lot going on right now. The worldwide pandemic took a piece out of all of us. When it feels like we're through, another variant raises its ugly head. Our kids and grandkids put their social activities and in-class learning on hold for two years. The solitary activity of sitting in front of a computer can never replace the interaction of learning from a teacher with friends in class.

Evelyn and I feel like the pandemic cheated us out of two years of our grandkids' lives. We all did our best under the circumstances. We would sit on the doorstep when our son and his family dropped by to visit at a distance. One day, as they were leaving, Evelyn held her arms out and said, "I'm giving you a virtual hug." Our grandson, six at the time, had heard about elderly people being at greater risk from the pandemic and said, "We can't hug you. You're too old." I guess we can consider ourselves elderly now.

We all lost at least two years of our lives.

Now that we are surfacing again, we're buffeted by rising costs, a shortage of products we took for granted before the pandemic, and anxiety over the insane war in Ukraine and other conflicts around the world. Misinformation is forcing us to question everything or go to dark places. Even as social gatherings reopened, it seemed people didn't know how to interact anymore. We're mad at all levels of government for doing too much or not enough, the health care system for the lack of treatment, available medicine, and hospital beds, the travel industry for losing our suitcase or messing up our vacation plans, our local grocery store clerk just because he or she is there…. The list goes on and on. People are angry. And that's only in the developed nations.

Blaming it all on the pandemic is a simple solution, but it doesn't make the problem go away. Nor does assigning labels to the angry masses. The world's leaders need to understand the anger and address it. People need to feel productive, that they are contributing to society, and that someone is listening. There is very little accountability for anything, nor are people willing to take responsibility. While the pandemic exacerbated the problem, the anger goes beyond that, and it needs to be addressed at the grassroots level. I'm not here to suggest solutions to that problem, but I am here to suggest that in the meantime, we all need inspiration from time to time to keep going.

Not to trivialize things, but let me give you a simple example of inspiration. Since I trained to climb Kilimanjaro, I tried to maintain my lifestyle through diet and exercise. I go to a gym because being around other people doing the same thing motivates me. People at the gym rarely talk to each other, although I greet a few regulars and wonder if there is a problem when they don't show up.

Sometimes, it seems like too much effort to get off the sofa and exercise, especially in the winter in Canada. It would be easier to sip a cup of coffee, check the news, do some writing, or anything other than get dressed, start the cold car, and head out to the gym. We need to keep going somehow.

That's when my favorite rock groups of the sixties come to mind.

Okay, stop laughing and let me finish. If you think about it, most surviving members of bands from that era are in their late seventies or early eighties now. Despite their alleged over-the-top lifestyles, many are still performing. Some of the lead singers sing and dance nonstop while racing from one side of the stage to the other for ninety minutes or more. Touring around the world must be exhausting. You may not like the music, but you have to admire the longevity, passion, stamina, and energy level that many still display at their age. Feeling energetic and enthusiastic at any age is something to which we all can and should aspire.

It makes getting up and going to the gym on a wintry day feel like something I should be able to do. I'm not drawing any comparisons between what they're doing and what I'm doing, other than being active at a certain age. Nobody wants to see me sing and dance for two minutes, let alone ninety. At least, I should be able to feel energized throughout the day, and exercise goes a long way toward achieving that goal.

We're all inspired by different things, and sometimes, we need a reminder about what others are doing or have done to give us the impetus to carry on. Some things that inspire us may seem weird to others, but that's okay. What works for us is what counts.

After coming up with the motto, "Every mountain top is within reach if you just keep climbing," many people suggested I should write a book about it. The climb itself has been documented in a book written by Chris and me called *Kilimanjaro and Beyond: A Life-Changing Journey*. I resisted the suggestions to write about the quote for a long time because I never considered myself qualified. Coming up with the motto was one thing. Writing an entire book about it without sounding self-indulgent or preachy was something completely different. Who am I to tell other people how they should live their lives? However, the suggestions grew louder when more and more people quoted the motto. It shocked me recently to learn that hundreds of people around the world have quoted it on social media and various knickknacks. It's simple, but it obviously means something to many people.

Visiting Africa twice taught me that we are all in this together. We all dream of a better future and face challenges. We need to do what we can to help ourselves, but we also need to do what we can to help others. Inspiring people shared their stories with me for this book, and if they will share openly and allow me to pass the stories on to you, it is time for me to do that.

CHAPTER THREE

THE DAY MY LIFE CHANGED

At 5,895 meters, or 19,340 feet, Mount Kilimanjaro is the highest mountain on the African continent. I'm extremely proud to have done the climb and as mentioned, it led to several changes in my life, including developing my motto, which I now apply to everything that happens on a day-to-day basis.

There are many people much older than me who have successfully made the climb. According to *the Guinness Book of Records*, the oldest man to climb is Fred Distelhorst, an American who completed it at eighty-eight years of age. The oldest woman to do it is American Anne Lorimor, who was eighty-nine. They are amazing people for having done the climb at their respective ages. I'm sure they are proud of their accomplishments, just as I am of mine. I should add that Coltan Tanner, from Albuquerque, New Mexico in the United States, received special permission to climb Kilimanjaro and accomplished it at age six! There will always be people who have done things at a younger or older age, climbed higher, dived deeper, had better marks, had more money…. Their accomplishments shouldn't change the satisfaction we feel from reaching our goals.

I can't say I dreamt of climbing a mountain. It wasn't something I always wanted to do or had even considered. I grew up on the flat Canadian prairies and didn't see a mountain, or even a large hill, until I was twelve years old when my aunt took me on a train through the Canadian Rockies. I remember staring at the gray and blue snow-capped peaks cemented against the cerulean sky with the green forests in the foreground. Add a pristine lake in front, and in my mind, you'll see nothing prettier. They're vistas ready to be painted, and as I discovered later, mountains whose cousin in Africa needed to be climbed. I was awestruck, and maybe somewhere back in the recesses of my mind, I wondered what it would be like to stand at the top.

In my twenties, I attended a presentation by Canadian mountain climber, Laurie Skreslet, about his climb of Mount Everest, and I'll admit his videos enthralled and stuck with me. He became the first Canadian to reach Everest's peak in 1982, but it still wasn't something I ever saw myself doing. In fact, it looked cold and miserable, and there were ladders and ropes involved. The climbers looked depleted, and it appeared they would have been much happier sitting in their living rooms watching TV. I'm not enthused about our Canadian winters, and to experience the wind and snow while standing unable to breathe on the raw edge of nothing didn't appeal to me. I admired him for doing it, and the celebration when they reached the top was inspiring. It just wasn't even on my radar, at least consciously.

Things changed with a visit to our family doctor in 2007. He advised me that over thirty years of a mostly sedentary lifestyle behind a desk had taken its toll and elevated my triglycerides. He shocked me when he expanded on his diagnosis to mention the potential consequences were a heart attack or stroke. I waited impatiently for him to get to the part where he would fix it, but it didn't come. Instead, he told me only *I* could fix it by changing my lifestyle through diet and exercise.

Our doctor's office was a thirty-minute drive to our house, and it gave me time to think, but, fortuitously, not enough time to change my mind. I altered my route slightly and ended up at a gym where I registered for a handful of sessions with a personal trainer. It turned out she was twenty-one years old and expected to get me to a point where I could do everything she could. Many nights after my workout, I would sit in the locker room with my head hanging, willing myself not to throw up.

My wife and I started eating healthier, and I continued working out. When the money ran out to work with the trainer, I still tried to do something every day, whether it was climbing the stairs to my office on the thirteenth floor, hiking in Quebec's Gatineau Park, or riding my bike. A miracle happened. At least, that's what I call it now. I lost twenty-eight pounds, my triglyceride levels dropped, and I had never felt better in my life. My trainer may not have gotten me to her twenty-one-year-old level of fitness and agility, but for me, it was a life-changing moment.

I pondered activities to pursue with my newfound energy, especially with my sixtieth birthday fast approaching. One of our sons, Chris, had mentioned climbing Africa's highest mountain about two years previously, and it must have stuck in the recesses of my mind. Maybe seeing the Rockies and hearing Laurie Skreslet's presentation had something to do with it, as well. I'll never know for sure, but I investigated Chris's suggestion. If ladders and ropes were to be involved, I would have had nothing to do with it. I talked to people who climbed Mount Kilimanjaro and read all the information available to discover it was a hike. Not an easy hike, but a hike, nonetheless. According to everyone I talked to who knew something about it, the wild card that would determine the outcome was the altitude. I broached the subject with Chris, who discussed it with his wife. They had a one-year-old daughter, so I imagine intense discussions took place, but I eventually received the phone call telling me he was in.

Then, I wondered what I had done.

The training continued, the days went by, and we headed off to Tanzania and the adventure of a lifetime.

Now, I often look back on our adventure and the changes that resulted. I consider each day since the climb a blessing. Every day presents an opportunity to try something new or to move something one step closer to completion. There are times in our lives when we receive a wakeup call, and realize we need to make the most of the life we have. That happened for me that day in the doctor's office. I realized I had one life to live. I had work to do to keep it going as long as possible, and I wanted to make the best of it.

EVERY DAY PRESENTS AN OPPORTUNITY TO TRY SOMETHING NEW OR TO MOVE SOMETHING ONE STEP CLOSER TO COMPLETION.

THE CHALLENGE
TO FOLLOW
OUR PASSION

CHAPTER FOUR

PASSION IS A DRIVING FORCE

Challenges arise no matter what we're doing. Let's take our career as an example. No matter the career choice we make, we will face challenges. There will be good times, and there will be stress. There will be times we just can't wait until retirement comes. Don't wish your life away. Retirement comes before we know it.

One of the driving forces for happiness in our work is passion. If we are passionate about what we do, it makes climbing above the challenges we face that much more interesting. Passion gives us more energy and makes us more innovative. We look forward to contributing. Based on my experience, being passionate about something makes the time go by much faster. My retirement came in the blink of an eye, and now that I'm passionate about writing and other interests, my retirement years are flying by as well. Kind of scary when I spend too much time pondering it, but I wouldn't want it any other way.

Many of us choose a career based on our education. When we're studying, we don't know for sure where it will take us. It isn't always passion that drives us toward a job. We choose a job that fits our educational background, and we hope we become at least somewhat passionate about the choice we made.

There's probably no one more passionate about their work than the person who assumes financial risk to own and operate a business, the entrepreneur. It takes a whole different breed to develop a business into something viable. I may be biased, but to me, farmers are the ultimate entrepreneurs. The families on Evelyn's side and mine are farmers. My dad was passionate about his work, and I'm sure he would have been happy if my three brothers and I had followed in his footsteps. He got two out of the four. My next oldest brother and I left the farm at the first opportunity. Both of us sought our passions somewhere else. The other two stayed and were passionate about what they did.

The farmer's office is his field. They must be adaptable to changing weather patterns, especially now with wild and unpredictable storms coming from nowhere. Flexibility is a prerequisite as fluctuating market prices and conditions force them to change crops and machinery. They must be innovative to switch things up when something isn't working. Dedication and willingness to work long hours are prerequisites. Mental toughness is required to meet all the challenges they face and to stay strong when everything seems to be against them.

Communication skills are required to negotiate with implement dealers and others. They must be intelligent to follow the markets and latest trends. Most of all, they must be passionate, or they wouldn't put themselves through everything required to be an entrepreneur. And through all that, they often don't receive the recognition they deserve.

There are innumerable other examples of passionate entrepreneurs. Our eldest son, Trevor, has been a singer/songwriter in Nashville for several years. He has always been passionate about music. In fact, he and his guitar were in the "couples" section of his high school yearbook. My wife and I had reservations about his career choice when he started, and after many discussions, we reluctantly agreed that he should "try it for a year."

He has experienced many challenges through his now lengthy career when he didn't know where his next nickel would come from. He busked on the street in the early years to pay the bills. He persevered when many others gave up and has since traveled the world doing what he loves. Passion has driven his career. He just kept climbing.

Not to be outdone, our second son, Christopher, is passionate about accounting. He had his turn as an entrepreneur. He started his own successful firm with several employees. It required long hours managing the employees and maintaining the overhead for the building occupied by his firm, all while keeping the clients happy. He continued to follow his passion for accounting until an offer came along from a top international accounting firm to buy his business. He is now a partner with the firm.

It doesn't matter what we're doing, we can be passionate about it. It could be flying a commercial airplane or shining shoes.

The notion about the wakeup call reminding us that we only have one life to live couldn't be clearer. We should follow our passion into our work if we're strong enough and can make a living at it. If we don't find our passion in our job, we should find it somewhere else. Play guitar, collect stamps, read, paint, work with wood, putter in the yard… whatever moves us. When we find our passion is when our second life begins. That's when we come alive. But be warned, when you find your passion, the time will race by. That's far superior to limping miserably through life. Staring in the mirror at your gray hair and wrinkles, wondering how you got so old while being able to say it's been an incredible ride with no regrets, is well worth it.

Sometimes, it takes a while to find our passion, but that's okay. I'm inspired by people who enjoy a successful career but discover a little something is still missing. You may know someone who has worked as a mechanic, for example, for several years before closing shop to become an actor. Or the welder whose actual passion is sculpting. I overheard a personal trainer in the gym say recently that money is great, but the ideal job is making fair cash and doing what you love. He had it right.

Jen Gilroy is such a person. She worked at a successful career in business before pursuing her ultimate passion as a full-time writer, demonstrating that dreams don't die. She kept her dream alive, and it's a lesson to us all. If your job is not quite what you would like it to be, read Jen's story for inspiration.

CHAPTER FIVE

THE COURAGEOUS CAREER CHANGER

I came across Jen Gilroy through a writing group we both belong to. I found out that she transitioned from a successful salaried career to write fiction full-time alongside caring for family. That's called taking a risk. Being kind of risk averse myself, at least with my livelihood, her story intrigued me, and I thought it could be inspirational to people who are considering something similar. This is Jen's story.

Jen Gilroy grew up in Winnipeg, Manitoba, Canada, as an only child whose parents had family roots on the prairies and in Eastern Ontario. From an early age, she loved having stories read to her and still remembers the excitement of learning to read for herself.

An important part of her childhood was spending summers with her mother's parents in a small Rideau Valley town close to Ottawa, Ontario, Canada and near where she now lives. As well as visiting her dad's small Manitoba hometown, those experiences were integral in shaping the small-town, rural fiction she now writes.

Growing up, Jen was a quiet, bookish, and sensitive child and adolescent. While that personality is ideal for a writer, it can make growing up and school life difficult. Since she often felt she didn't fit in, fiction, both reading and writing it, offered escape when things were hard.

Books helped her find new ways of seeing and being in the world beyond her own life, and she discovered other people like her, too. Along with her parents and grandparents, librarians at school and in the community were important in her young life and in helping her navigate the path to adulthood.

In some ways, Jen's experiences growing up made her an observer and listener and helped her develop empathy, all of which are also essential to writing fiction.

Jen had a varied career spanning academia, government, and corporate communications, as well as editing, marketing, and international business development. Still, she can't remember a time when she didn't write. As a child, she had her own mini newspaper and was always scribbling stories and poems. When university and adult life happened, her writing related by necessity to her studies and then, work. Writing fiction took a back seat for many years.

Like most people, life has thrown challenges at Jen. From bereavements to tough career situations, family and personal tragedies, wrong choices, and more, she's tried to see life's challenges as learning opportunities. She talks of the mindset she's always had that if she can't go around obstacles, one way or another and by sheer grit, she will persevere through them.

She just keeps climbing, adding that ice cream and a sense of humor help.

After some significant life losses, she found solace in creative writing and started working seriously towards writing fiction for traditional publication. Jen started writing full time in late 2015, and it's a decision that evolved. After many years of living and working in England, she took voluntary redundancy from her job because she and her family wanted to return to live in Canada. Her family caregiving responsibilities increased. Since those took priority, writing gave her the flexibility she needed to balance work and family life.

Soon after returning to Canada in 2015, she signed her first traditional publishing deal (in romance), and her writing career has developed since then. While books and writing have always been part of her life, after a varied and international career, living the author's life has brought her full circle to who, what, and where she wanted to be as a child. She continues to do other ad hoc freelance work around writing, but writing is now her primary job. She currently writes romance for Harlequin Heartwarming and historical women's fiction.

As in all jobs, the author's life has difficulties, but Jen appreciates her husband's and daughter's support for her career change and her writing. She had a long writing apprenticeship with help from other authors and a professional body called the Romantic Novelists' Association (RNA) New Writers Scheme (NWS) in the U.K. Through the RNA and NWS, she found her first writing community and close friends with whom she continues to share ups and downs in writing and life. Thanks to the RNA and annual NWS manuscript critiques she received from multi-published, experienced authors, Jen learned the craft and business of writing and publishing, which helped her become traditionally published. Now, as a published, full RNA member, and alongside her agents and publishers, she continues to value that community in helping her navigate and develop her author career.

Like most writers, and especially when rejections arrive, which don't stop once published, Jen often considered giving up on writing. She readily admits that, to a certain extent, each book she writes is a struggle, and at the mid-point in particular, it can be a challenge to keep going. Self-doubt creeps in too, but she perseveres and keeps writing because she loves crafting stories and has many more she wants to tell.

From childhood, she'd dreamed of being a traditionally published author—unlike today, that was almost the only way to publish—and seeing her books on library shelves. Whenever tempted to give up on her writing dream, she realized if she didn't keep trying, she'd reach the end of her life with regrets. Another writer once told her that the only difference between a published and unpublished author is that the published one didn't stop trying. That motivated her to persevere in the face of rejection and other setbacks.

For anyone considering taking a risk with their career path, Jen's story is truly inspirational. The last words go to her about how her life has changed because of the risks she took and the choices she made.

My life has changed immeasurably and largely for the better. While I'm not as well-off financially, I've been able to be a caregiver for various family members when needed, juxtaposing such "labours of love" around my writing career.

As someone whose life was once dominated by the corporate nine-to-five and filled with international business travel, I now work from home and, to some extent, can set my schedule. That gives me a much better balance between work and family life.

I also have less stress (no more "Sunday evening scaries"!), am more physically active, and consciously take time to breathe and practice gratitude.

As an introvert, working from home on my own suits me too. The one downside? With my work footwear now composed largely of slippers or sensible footwear for walking the dog, I sometimes miss the stylish shoes that were once a daily wardrobe staple. Now packed away in boxes and only worn infrequently, they're ghosts of a past life I remember fondly, but at least on a full-time basis, don't want to revisit.

You can find Jen Gilroy's contemporary romance and Second World War/dual timeline historical women's fiction on Amazon and from other retailers.

THE RESILIENT
BODY BUILDER

Jen Gilroy always knew what her passion was from the time she was a little girl. She took the risk of pursuing her dream. Others discover their passion out of necessity.

Gabriella Varga has been a family friend for several years. She's a first-generation Canadian whose parents immigrated from Europe in the 1960s. Her father escaped the Hungarian Revolution, and her mother moved to Canada to support her brother while he started a business. Her mom and dad met in a small mining town named Elliot Lake in northern Ontario, Canada. Because both parents lived through the end of World War II, things were scarce growing up, including food. The family didn't waste any. Gabriella ate what her parents put on her plate. If she didn't eat supper, it was there for breakfast, and she ate nothing else until it was gone.

It was a very strict home, and when the time came for Gabriella to go for post-secondary education in nursing, she had to leave town and move to Sudbury, Ontario, the nearest city two hours away. Growing up, she didn't have the luxury of eating out or having treats in the house, so when she went away to school, she admits she definitely indulged! Not only was she eating badly, but the stress of going to school and working was tipping her over the edge. Her parents couldn't afford to pay for her schooling. She received money from the Ontario Student Assistance Program, but she also had to work to make ends meet. During her second year of nursing when she was nineteen, Gabriella's father passed away from a chronic illness. She had quit school early so she could help care for her dad. That left her one course short to complete her second year.

Losing her father on March 8th, 1995, left her depleted, and she just didn't have it in her to go back to school that year. The next summer she moved to Ottawa, Ontario, and one day, after reapplying to nursing school at Algonquin College, she looked into the sky and said, "Dad, if it's meant to be, I'll get in." A week later, she received the phone call with the good news that class would start in two weeks.

Gabriella couldn't afford her first semester tuition. Her mom helped as much as she could, but Gabriella had to work nights at Tim Horton's to pay for rent and food while trying to save money for the next year's tuition. She would go to class from 8:00 A. M. to 4:00 P. M., return home and sleep until 9:00 P. M., work the night shift from 11:00 P. M to 7:00 A. M., only to go home to shower and be back in class by 8:00. It must have been an incredibly hard two years.

Some say that kind of schedule would make you a stronger person, but Gabriella always felt she was one step behind

everybody else. She swore when she graduated that if she ever had children, she would make sure they didn't have to do what she did to finish school. She says that because of her schedule, her nutrition was terrible. Horrible sleep patterns, no time to take care of herself, let alone exercise, and at the end of that journey, she weighed around 220 pounds.

It had to be discouraging because she was quite athletic in her teen years. She was a competitive gymnast and on every sports team that she could get on. Gabriella admits she was never the skinny athletic type, always heavier set despite everything she tried. She describes herself as a professional Yo-Yo dieter... lose a little, gain a little... trying whatever new trending diet that came along. She was always a little successful too, losing five or ten pounds, but never able to lose the weight she wanted, nor keep it off.

At one point, she joined a diet company and lost eighty pounds. She had never been happier with her success, but just like every other time, the weight slowly crept back to where she was teetering on 242 pounds. She had no self-esteem, her confidence was nonexistent, and to add to her situation, she was in an abusive marriage.

She recalled a line in a poem she used to read when she was little. "When things were good, they were very, very good, but when things were bad, they were horrid." That's how she describes her marriage. She always used to think it wasn't her husband's fault. He didn't know any better since his dad was much worse towards his mom. It was during her marriage that she found solace in running. It got her out of the house a few days a week. She describes herself as a "master compartmentalizer." She focused on other things, so she didn't have to deal with issues at home. She recounts the time during her marriage:

Today I am thankful for my hardship because it made me stronger, and more confident, and it made me believe that I truly can accomplish anything when I set my mind to it. I remember one day twelve years into my marriage and two beautiful babies later, having coffee with my girlfriend and her telling me she was going to leave her husband. The news gassed me. I always thought they had a good marriage, but she confided in me that behind closed doors, he wasn't very nice to her. Her words resonated with me more than any words I had ever heard when she said, 'I don't want my daughter to think it's normal to be treated this way.'

I thought, oh my God, I did not want my girls to think the marriage I was in was normal. God, I never want them to experience anything like I had been going through for the last twelve years. My friend's words stuck to me like glue over the next few months, and my husband and I had one last fight. I remember that day like it was yesterday. Shaking with terror, I grabbed my daughters and not a thing more. I ran to my car and didn't even put the girls in their car seats. I locked the doors and drove to the nearest store parking lot with people all around. I parked the car, trembling in fear, strapped the girls in, and called my friend. I needed a place to stay for a couple of days. Wow, I thought things were rough in my marriage. Now what? I was a single-mom, overweight, out of shape, easily out of breath, and struggling to keep up with my two little girls.

Gabriella had lost a couple of pounds running, but she was still battling obesity, and now, she was down to one income. She found out the experts aren't lying when they say it's expensive to be healthy. Things were just that much harder, and the last thing she wanted to do was look at herself in the mirror. Years and years passed, and like she did previously, she hopped on the newest trendy diet and lost a few pounds, but after a few weeks, she'd seen only minor successes.

Five years after being on her own with the girls, she met Paul, an amazing man who showed her and the girls what a genuine relationship looked like. He stuck with her through the difficulties, and there were many. Her divorce was not an easy one. Paul also struggled with obesity, but he never voiced it like Gabriella. He joined her on all the "crazy diets," except the last. He balked at eating just eggs for days at a time. He drew the line. She ate just eggs for five days, followed by a week of no carbs, then back to eggs. The proponents of the diet called it a fast. The egg diet was Gabriella's last diet trend.

After starving on a diet of approximately 700 calories a day, Gabriella was truly fed up. She recognized she needed help, and a friend suggested a lifestyle coach. The friend connected her with an organization dedicated to helping women lose weight and improve their fitness. After researching the organization, Gabriella connected with the coach, who was a Canadian champion bikini competitor, and her true journey began.

I started my self-improvement journey in January 2020, and my coach gave me a fitness and meal plan. It focused on losing weight so I could have more energy for the girls and an easier time moving. Who knew if you ate more and moved a little, you would lose weight? Isn't that an oxymoronic thought? Have we not always been told that to lose weight you have to eat less (go on a diet)?

Never in my lifetime did I ever think that I could lose weight by eating more. More carbohydrates. More fats. More protein. Geez, every diet I've ever been on, they told me to eat fewer carbs, eat less fat. But wow, did it ever work!

After consistently working with her trainer for a year, Gabriella lost a hundred pounds. She felt great. She had energy and confidence. She wanted to tell the world, to share everything she had learned with anyone who would listen.

Throughout her journey, she set small goals, but never anything food related. She learned that food was fuel for the body, not an emotion. She set a big goal for herself when she hit the one hundred pounds lost mark. She wanted to have a professional photo shoot. She found a photographer in Montreal, where she spent the day getting her hair and makeup done, changing into five or six different outfits, and posing, laughing, and having the most amazing time. Then her coach asked what the next goal was, and she realized she didn't have one. Her fitness competitor coach asked if she ever thought of competitive bodybuilding.

It was something Gabriella had thought of as a teen, but still lacking confidence, she asked if it was really something she could do. Her coach said, "Absolutely, there's no reason you couldn't. Look how far you've come. If we work a few more weeks together, I can get you ready for the stage." Gabriella talked to her partner and daughters, since they'd already had to deal with the last year of her "crazy exercise and meal preps." They all agreed she should try.

She didn't start her journey thinking she wanted to be a bodybuilder, but that's where it led her. It was not a simple journey. She never wanted the experience to interfere with her family. At the beginning of her first competition prep, she was an intensive care nurse at the peak of the pandemic. She worked twelve-hour shifts two days in a row, followed by two nights, and then five days off. She pointed out that five days off sounds great, but she spent the first two recovering from post-night fatigue, which becomes more difficult as you get older. Her day shift started at 7:00 A.M., and toward the end of her prep, she was doing close to two hours of cardio a day. Some mornings she had to get up at 3:30 A.M. to be in the gym early enough to get her cardio done, because she had another hour of weight training after her twelve-hour shift.

Gabriella admits that working out after a twelve-hour night shift was brutal, but she committed to succeeding, so she thought she had no option. She said, "Bless my family, is all I have to say, especially my partner, Paul." Paul supported her in her quest by helping to prep meals. She acknowledges she was cranky and had little patience. She added, "I don't think I can thank them enough for their love, support, kindness, and patience even when I had none."

When she thought of giving up, she would stand on the scale. She made it to 13% body fat and lost 117 pounds in total. She had never seen the scale that low, even as a teen. She would see something new in her muscle definition, or a vein pop, and it was enough to encourage her to push harder. Her daughters would remind her how amazing her muscles looked, and that made her push harder. Podcasters would mention that, statistically, only 1% of the population have the drive to compete in fitness competition prep, and that made her push harder. Thinking that she was about to stand on stage with women ten years younger, who had been in fitness their whole lives, pushed her harder. People at work noticed the changes in her physique. She concluded that her love language was words of affirmation.

When I asked if she rewarded herself after milestones, she pointed out that when you're on a weight loss journey, rewarding yourself becomes very different. Since food would defeat the purpose, she found other healthy rewards. She didn't trust herself with food for fear of restarting a binging behavior. Facials, manicures, pedicures, and massages became her reward. Clothes were out of the question since her body was always changing, but shoes always fit. She proclaimed, "You should see my collection!"

Gabriella's journey has been a very personal one, but it not only changed her life, it changed everyone's lives in her family. Bodybuilding is not necessarily a healthy sport, so since her last show, she has been working with a naturopath doctor to get her hormones back on track. She says, "Let's be honest, I'm not in my prime anymore," but she keeps climbing. She's still in the gym six days a week. I recall seeing her in the gym one morning around nine A.M., and she told me it was her second visit that day! Gabriella still has a coach, and they're working on improving her physique to prepare for the next show to bring an even better package to the stage. Today, she gets excited when she makes personal records on the heaviest lifts. Each success brings a reward, so she says she has way too many shoes.

Her partner, Paul, has now lost over a hundred pounds. The couple love to hike and do outdoor activities together. Gabriella's oldest daughter, Paige, started going to the gym with her and competed alongside her in the last two competitions. She now has the bug and is training for her third competition.

Her youngest daughter, Kiera, might not have found the fitness bug, but she has become creative in the kitchen helping with meal preps and has found a new joy in cooking healthy meals for the family. She is contemplating going into culinary arts now.

Gabriella has become a board member for a women's only bodybuilding federation in Ottawa. It's a non-profit organization dedicated to showcasing women's success in both physical and mental transformations. She says that being a part of such a wonderful organization has truly been an amazing experience. She has told her story on Canadian Broadcasting Corporation (CBC) radio and presented at the Ottawa National Women's Show, educating other women on the importance of nutrition and health. She hopes to support more women in reaching their health goals. More information on the organization is available at www. womenscommunityofbodybuilding.com.

After everything she went through, the strict upbringing, difficult marriage, money problems, crazy hours, and struggling with obesity, on September 11th, 2021, at forty-five years of age, Gabriella Varga walked onto the stage for the first time. She trembled in fear, anxiousness, and excitement. She cried back-stage when they told her fitness story and called her name. She showcased her success and won first place in all three categories she competed in. She proved to herself, her family, and her friends that if you commit to a process, anything is possible. All the sacrifices she made, parties she missed, and events she brought cold chicken and broccoli to, were worth that five minutes on stage. She was a winner!

CHALLENGING OURSELVES PHYSICALLY

CHAPTER SEVEN

WHY DO WE
DO THIS?

Jen Gilroy challenged herself to change her career. Gabriella Varga challenged herself to improve her lifestyle. Both had their reasons and were inspired to do so. Some like to give themselves physical challenges to go where few others have gone before or to do something few others have done. Those who don't gravitate toward physical challenges may ask why anyone would put themselves through that.

It's a good question. Seriously, why would anyone climb a mountain? It's the age-old debate. The stock answer of, "because it's there," just doesn't seem to cut it. Why would anyone put themselves through the physical exertion required to reach a peak or any other physical challenge for that matter? We've read Gabriella's story and her reasons for bodybuilding. In the ensuing chapters you'll read about a seventy-year-old sprinter and an ultra-marathoner. Training every day, and often more than once a day, to race 400 meters doesn't sound like fun, does it? Why does anyone run ultra-marathons in extreme heat or cold? I can only address the mountain climbing question. I'll leave it to others to describe the challenges they gave themselves and how and why they kept climbing in the following chapters.

Over ten years after my climb, I've had plenty of time to reflect on the question. Why did we do it? Initially, it was because I wanted to challenge myself, and after considering other possibilities, it seemed to be the right thing to do, or at least to try. Reaching the top was the goal, but there were so many variables there could be no guarantee we would succeed. As I look back, whipping my body into the best shape of my life was the big goal. Reaching the top of Africa's highest mountain was icing on the cake and confirmation that we had succeeded. Little did I know, there would be lots of other desserts to savor along the way that would enrich my life. I'll call those desserts the five Ps. Persistence. Patience. Preservation. Perspective. Pride.

Everything we do is a learning opportunity, and the mountain taught me so much. It's a massive hunk of rock rising from the ground on the borders of Kenya and Tanzania. It's the highest, free-standing mountain in the world, unable to comprehend that it's teaching everyone who climbs it valuable lessons about life. The same goes for every mountain, whether it is an enormous piece of rock or some other life challenge thrown in our direction.

The five Ps are the payoff for all the hard work that goes into climbing any mountain. Most apply to any challenge we give ourselves. To help understand why people challenge themselves, let's examine the five Ps.

Persistence was required to prepare for the climb. I joined my trainer two or three times a week, and some days, I was still sore from the previous session when it was time to go again. Some days, it was an effort to push myself out the door. Persistence paid off as it led Chris and me to base camp at the foot of the mountain, ready for the climb on day one.

We discovered that the need for persistence wasn't over. Far from it. As we climbed through the intense heat of the rainforest, over and around rocks, slipped on volcanic shale, and tried to breathe as we hunkered down in the icy wind, we learned we had to persist if we were going to reach the top. It was a matter of putting one foot in front of the other. A tight band formed around my head around the 16,000-foot mark, and breathing became labored. Our heart rates rose as we climbed, and oxygen levels dropped. Chris felt even worse with his altitude sickness and knee injury. Our fellow climber, Peter Yates, had a torn ligament in his calf muscle.

Setbacks are an undeniable part of any challenge. At one point, I lost my breath completely and asked the guides and my fellow climbers to stop for a few seconds until I could breathe again. I was proud of myself for not panicking. Evelyn likes to quote the Persian adage, "This too shall pass," and it did.

We all persisted throughout the climb. After summiting, we had to have oxygen to replenish the supply our bodies needed. The adventure challenged us, but that's why we were there. We persisted, and we made it. More than ever, when setbacks pop up, we have to just kept climbing.

Persistence applies to everything. When a challenge seems too great, we need to persist to reach our objectives. As we learned with Jen and Gabriella and will soon learn from others, persistence is a key to overcoming challenges.

A second valuable lesson was **patience**. Countless times each day, we heard the words, "pole, pole," (pronounced pole-lay) from our Swahili-speaking Tanzanian guides. It's a reminder to proceed slowly, slowly, and that's how we climbed. At times, we thought we could have gone faster, but our guides held us back, and for good reason. Success comes to those who take their time climbing, so they can adapt to the altitude changes.

A mountain hiking strategy calls for climbing high and sleeping low. The day before the final ascent, we arrived at the last camp around noon, expecting to enjoy an afternoon rest. It wasn't to be. Our guides insisted on another 1,000-foot climb in freezing cold and wind to acclimatize. So, before resting, we pushed through the weather, fatigue, and labored breathing to climb up 1,000 feet and down 1,000 feet.

Patience applies to everything we do. Some things take longer than others, and we need to respect that. I must admit, the lesson about patience still evades me. When I talk about age and patience, I like to say I have too much of one and not enough of the other. I still like most things to be done yesterday. We're constantly learning, right?

The third lesson the mountain taught us is **preservation**. I mean this in two ways. The first lesson was to preserve our strength to the extent possible as we climbed and to ensure we chose qualified, well-trained guides who would do their best to do the same with our well-being. It was a lesson to preserve mind, body, and spirit.

We also observed the diversity of Mother Nature and received a valuable lesson on humankind's responsibility to preserve it. Climbers on Mount Kilimanjaro experience an incredible five ecological zones. Each of the zones can be referred to as beautiful, but that would be redundant. We traveled in the enclosed back of a truck for six hours divided equally into good road, bumpy road, and virtually no road to arrive at our starting point. Travel books refer to the area we passed through as bushland, although the locals have turned much of it into farmland. The truck's grimy plastic window coverings obscured our view, but we spotted some plantations and orchards. The guides identified them as either bananas, fruit, or coffee. Rainfall is abundant in this area, and the farmers also rely on the runoff from the snow and glaciers on the mountain.

The first day of hiking is through a dense, humid rainforest that made the sweat pop. We pushed through the lush greenery that closed in from both sides of the hiking trail as the prickly leaves grabbed at our clothes. Colobus monkeys howled and yapped to each other at daybreak. Once through the rainforest, we arrived at a cooler, open area which reminded us of the moorlands of Scotland. Not much grows except heathers and moss. A harsh, desolate zone follows where the difference between daylight and nighttime temperatures fluctuates wildly. No wildlife apparent except the odd spider. Rocks of various shapes and sizes lay strewn about, heaved haphazardly by a series of volcanic eruptions over the years. The volcano is dormant but still active, so potential for another eruption still exists. The final zone is called the Arctic zone for good reason. It is gray, ash covered, and barren. Winds rippled our clothing as we hunkered our chins into the necks of our coats and kept putting one foot in front of the other.

An image that is burned into my memory forever occurred as we finished our evening meal in the mess tent on day five. As we climbed, we didn't really have a sense of our destination. We trudged along, often staring at the heels of the person in front of us or peering through the mist and clouds, trying to see the flag showing our stopping point for the day. Clouds or mist often obscured our view when we did look up.

After our meal, we stepped out of the mess tent. The sky had cleared, and the craggy top of Kilimanjaro with the sun glistening off the glaciers greeted us. The wind whipped snow clouds into the air at the peak against the backdrop of the bright blue sky. I had to swallow hard against the lump in my throat caused by the sight in front of us.

Each of the zones is magnificent in its own way and a reminder that humanity must be aware of and actively take part in its preservation. There is no starker reminder than the glaciers near the top of Kilimanjaro. When we were there, open fields had replaced much of the glacial ice. I suspect it is worse now, and if the glaciers disappear completely, the runoff will no longer be available to the farmers who rely on it.

Having seen photos from the past of the giant glaciers at the top of Kilimanjaro and comparing them to what we saw compels me to briefly address the touchy subject of global warming. There are those who argue it doesn't exist, that changing weather patterns are a cyclical phenomenon and people have no impact. Among those who believe humanity contributes to global warming will be some who point out the harmful effects of airplane travel, that the plane that took us to Tanzania spewed contrails of greenhouse gases into the air and contributed to noise pollution. On the flip side, by staying in Tanzania, we contributed to their economy and provided employment for the locals who guided us up the mountain. Thanks to our climb, we raised money for four projects to help the children of Tanzania.

Although I'm skeptical, global warming may turn out to be cyclical, and years from now, the earth will be back to where it was. In the meantime, surely there can be no harm in working together to try to shorten the cycle of harsh weather patterns we're currently experiencing to preserve what we have, reduce property damage, and most of all, save lives. One could argue the various sides endlessly, so I'll leave it at that.

The next lesson learned was **perspective**. Whatever the challenge may be, we are looking at it from the perspective of someone who is doing something we haven't done before. Others may have undertaken the same challenge, and we can rely on them for inspiration or guidance, but for us, it's something new. As we climbed through the various ecological zones, we saw sights that not everyone has seen. I can say the same for when we stood at the peak. Chris, our fellow climber, Peter Yates, and I may have had a different perspective on how it felt to reach our goal, but we had one thing in common. We all looked down on the clouds from the perspective of three people who were doing something for the first time, something that most people will never do.

The same goes for anything we do in life. New challenges bring us a fresh perspective. Maybe thousands of others have undertaken the same challenge, but it brings a new perspective for us. We should be proud of our accomplishment when we conquer the challenge and relish in our success.

The last lesson the mountain gave us is, of course, **pride**. We worked for more than a year to reach the top, and we did it! We only spent fifteen to twenty minutes at the top, but it was enough to contribute to vast changes in my life. Changes in the way I think, changes in the way I approach things, changes in lifestyle, and changes in what I wanted to do for the rest of my life all came about because of that climb. Above all, the mountain taught me to just keep climbing, no matter what the challenge may be, and to be proud of my success. A reward to celebrate any success is always in order, even if it's just a virtual pat on the back, and we should never let other people's accomplishments detract from the pride we feel for what we have done.

Any challenge gives us the same learning opportunities, whether or not we realize it. Persistence to overcome the challenge. Patience to work our way through it. Preserving our strength to fight the battles worth winning. Fresh perspective from overcoming a new challenge and the experience, knowledge, and understanding to take on the next one. And finally, pride knowing we can do it, which gives us the strength to keep on climbing.

It's time to hear from two ladies who have given themselves challenges that go far and above what most people will face in their lives. They pushed the boundaries to step outside their comfort zones. As you read their stories, think about how the five Ps apply. While their accomplishments are something that most of us will never achieve, their stories show us we can do whatever we want to do with hard work. They set goals for themselves and reached them. And they continue to set more… to push the limits.

Of course, when we set challenging goals, doubts can creep in. We'll ask ourselves if we're up to completing the task. I suspect these two women may not have uttered the words out loud, but at the very least, they silently asked and answered themselves.

Meet Karla Del Grande and Karen Meades, two very inspirational women.

CHAPTER EIGHT

THE DETERMINED SPRINTER

A headline caught my attention as I was scrolling through the news on the internet one day. It was an article in *Canadian Running Magazine* by Marley Dickinson, dated April 2023. It read in bold print, "Canada's Karla Del Grande sets two world records at masters events." I was immediately drawn to the article. Two world records! Being a proud Canadian, I had to read more about Karla, and I learned that she has set twelve records indoors and nine outdoors since 2004 in various age groups and events. She still holds four indoor records and three outdoors. Even more fascinating!

But what intrigued me the most was the word "masters." It implied that Karla had done something special at an age when most of us would prefer to sit on the sofa, reading. The article revealed that the Toronto sprinter had smashed world records in the 200m and 400m races in the 2023 World Masters Athletics Championships Indoors in Torun, Poland.

Organizers clocked her at an amazing twenty kilometers per hour (about twelve miles per hour) in the 400m! That's how Karla celebrated her seventieth birthday.

I reached out to Karla, and she generously shared her story; one that could lift anyone off the couch to do something physical at any age. Read her story for inspiration to get moving.

Karla Del Grande grew up with two active parents, in Burlington, Ontario, Canada. Both parents loved camping, square dancing, cross-country skiing, and lots of walking. They always involved their three children (Karla and her two younger brothers). Almost every day after work, if the weather was good, her dad would race them to the next telephone pole or play ball with neighborhood kids of all ages in the park across the street. It was motivation for the three siblings to have success running or in track and field events at school. Karla and one of her brothers joined a track club in their mid-teens and competed in mostly local or provincial meets.

Karla continued participating in various meets until she went to university, where she also competed in her first year. When life got in the way, she stopped training and competing, but was still active as she raised her daughter and worked at a career in teaching. She coached students in cross-country running and track and field and taught some physical education classes over the years.

Karla discovered that adding training for athletics to other expectations and roles in life is challenging for anyone, especially women. A single parent for many years, she experienced a busy, all-consuming teaching career, and later, two aging parents needing care. She pointed out that other women may have issues with pregnancy, hormones, or menopause as they age, so balancing life with training and physical challenges is difficult. Over the years, she balanced her challenges with finding time and energy for physical activity. She considered it important for her physically, emotionally, and mentally, and she was determined to figure things out. She would do lots of activity with her students, fit other things in before and after school, and make sure she focused her time to train and made it worthwhile.

When Karla was about forty-nine, she started in masters running doing road races, since that's what she assumed adults did if they wanted to run. To put this into perspective, Canadian Masters Athletics defines a masters runner as thirty-five and over. McMillan Running, a website dedicated to coaching runners, adds, "… all masters need to know their weaknesses…. Muscles, tendons and fascia grow stiff as we age. The masters runner needs to keep all his or her parts moving, supple, and in good working order."

Karla went with a colleague on weekly runs at a local running store, The Running Room, a family-owned company founded by John Stanton in 1984. The Running Room originally filled a niche in the running shoe marketplace by opening a small, one-room store in the renovated living room of an old house in Edmonton, Alberta, Canada. The stores have since expanded to over eighty locations across Canada and the United States.

It was a way for Karla to keep fit, active, and busy when her daughter had gone off to college, but she still had to fit training into the rest of her life. She wasn't aware of sprinting or track and field for older adults until she went to a speed training session for road races, such as the 10K and marathons. She loved the track workouts, and when someone told her about masters track and field, she investigated, found meets, and started sprint training with a coach at around fifty years of age. It was something she really wanted to do, to get better, and to see where it could take her.

She thought of quitting at times. She candidly admits that, whenever physical issues arise as a masters athlete which may affect one's training, she asked herself if her body was saying, "Wait a minute, what do you think you're doing at your age?" Karla answered the question of quitting this way:

> *In any gathering of masters athletes, when talk comes around to issues and injuries, you soon realize that EVERYONE has a laundry list of aches and pains, some minor, some majorly debilitating, that make you wonder how they even get out of bed in the morning, let alone sprint or pole vault or long jump. So, you get the required treatment and carry on because it's become a part of you that you can't imagine living without.*

As for setting goals, Karla says she enjoys the training more than the actual competing. She enjoys seeing and experiencing the progress of getting stronger and faster, but of course, she has to prove it to others in a race. She doesn't base her goals so much on specific numbers, but on getting better, so they are ever-changing. Masters athletes compare themselves to a standard which is expressed as a percentage of what they could have done as a younger elite athlete. A good goal is maintaining an age grading over 90 or 95%. Karla rewards herself by maintaining her age grading in that range and not losing speed as she ages. That's what keeps her "climbing."

Karla has set records in masters athletics and wants to set

the bar high for those women coming after to achieve. She wants them to look at the records and try to beat them. To do that, they **will** need to train hard, maybe harder than Karla. She credits her coach, Jamal Miller, who sees her age as one aspect of Karla the athlete. She looks at what's ahead, and he provides the workouts to help her achieve her goals.

Like all the inspiring people in this book, family plays an important part in Karla's life. Her daughter is extremely proud, and her very supportive husband does her travel planning and keeps her grounded at meets. Karla and her daughter ran a 5K together, which mom says was lots of fun but not so much for daughter. She's more inclined to yoga and has rock climbed, wrestled, cross-country skied, and biked over the years.

Karla trains at a facility for children and adults of all abilities called Variety Village. When she sees kids with cerebral palsy, artificial limbs, or in wheelchairs, or other adults undergoing rehab for accidents or strokes, she says she can't help but feel that she's doing what she does for them because she can. She wants to show what older women can do, for example, running at her age in the 400 meters. She's done it twice, the only known woman to do so (she completed it in sixty-eight seconds when she was sixty-eight and in sixty-nine seconds at sixty-nine).

I asked Karla who and what inspires her to "keep climbing" and how her lifestyle has changed because of the choices she has made. This is her response:

I'd love to keep going into my 90s as one of my heroes did ahead of me, Olga Kotelko, who started competing in athletics (running, jumping, throwing) when she was seventy-seven. There are many other female heroes ahead of me, several who are Canadian also, who have set the bar high in records and longevity... Carol Lafayette-Boyd, Christa Bortignon and Diane Palmason. I think my primary inspiration is to show what women can do at age sixty, sixty-five, and seventy. I like to surprise people who see a grey-haired teacher-librarian (what I was in my past life, and I think how I still appear), when they see I can also run. Not just run road races, but sprint.

My life revolves around my training to a great degree, which is my choice. So, that has changed me to be disciplined and focused. I still make time for family and other activities that I enjoy, such as reading and hiking with friends. I also enjoy working with our organization of Canadian Masters Athletics to encourage others to participate, which certainly has evolved from competing as a way to give back and enable others to experience the fun, fitness, and friendships that we see as the main benefits of our sport. So, my lifestyle choice led me to that.

Being inspired is one thing, but what's really important is that we take that inspiration or motivation and act on it. Then we'll form the habits that become our routine, and that's the motivation to keep going. Basically, we're all the same... trying to be the best versions of ourselves and to keep moving.

CHAPTER NINE

THE TENACIOUS
ULTRA-MARATHONER

I met Karen Meades through a mutual friend. Karen's story is so compelling, I had to reach out immediately. There are a couple of similarities between Karen's story and mine. We are both Chartered Professional Accountants, and we both climbed Mount Kilimanjaro. That's where the similarities end.

At fifty-nine years of age, Karen is actively training for the Britannia Rat Race, a 1,600 km (994 mile) run the entire length of the U.K. at 50km (31 miles) per day for thirty-five days. In 2018, she finished the last of the Four Deserts Race Series, which is widely recognized as the most prestigious outdoor footrace series in the world. It comprises the Sahara Race (Egypt), Gobi March (China), Atacama Crossing (Chile), and The Last Desert (Antarctica). Oh, and she has completed the swim from Alcatraz to the Bay of San Francisco. She did all of this while completing more degrees and accreditations, running her own consulting firm, and serving in various volunteer capacities.

Karen is truly inspirational.

She was born and raised in Montreal in a somewhat traditional Italian family way. She lived in a duplex with her grandmother on one level, her parents, brother, and her on the upstairs level, and her three unmarried uncles on the lower level. Interacting with all these adults daily offered access to many perspectives on life.

Most notable was her mom who would repeat something of a mantra. She would say, "You can do anything," instilling in Karen that anything was possible; it was just a matter of hard work. As she grew up, Karen realized that not *everything* is possible. As a child, you really see anything as possible in your mind's eye and believe it for a long time before life sets natural limitations. For Karen, it was an excellent beginning to what would become a life filled with wonderful, incredible adventures.

Karen met her first big challenge at school. She understood the importance of an education but didn't grasp why or how it worked. Fortunately, her grade eleven high school teacher, Mr. Whitey, suggested that since she was good at math, she should consider accounting as a profession. Mr. Whitey pointed Karen towards becoming a Chartered Accountant (now Chartered Professional Accountant, or CPA) just as my aunt did for me, and like me, she didn't know what a C.A. was, but pursued it anyway. As Karen points out, "There are kids who hear an adult offering advice, but you listen, or you don't listen. I had the great fortune of listening to Mr. Whitey."

Earning her CPA designation filled in a piece to a puzzle theory taught by one of her university professors, which Karen uses to this day to establish a balanced life. The professor drew a pie divided into eight equal parts for her students. She told the students that each piece represents an important part of life and that they should work on each one and put them all together. It was a life-changing moment for Karen.

The pieces of the pie described by Karen's professor are business/career, finances, health, family and friends, romance, personal growth, fun and recreation, and physical environment. The theory was that the students were to jot down thoughts as they came into their heads to fill in each piece of the puzzle. For example, if they heard someone say something about a career that seemed interesting, they jotted it down in that section of the pie. But that was it. Write it down and walk away. Let it ruminate for a while. For a balanced life, something should be written in each section of the pie.

Karen said, "The most amazing thing happened. Have you ever noticed when you buy, say a Honda, you are driving around in your new car, and suddenly, you see so many of the same vehicles on the road? You never saw them before, and now, every one of them is catching your attention."

Karen chose six of the pieces to represent her life, and every time she heard something that piqued her interest, she would write it down. She used the theory every day. In the category she called health, she jotted down the word, marathon. At the time, marathon running seemed to her to be for crazy people. The one picture that kept imposing itself in her mind was of someone super skinny crossing the finish line, collapsing, and looking near death. And of course, marathons were intended for fast runners, athletes. Well, like the Honda metaphor, once she jotted it down and left it alone for a while, she heard more and more about marathons. The pie chart became her way of goal setting. The chart remained fluid, but the ideas came together when opportunities presented themselves. She thought it was funny how she had written the word marathon, then started hearing marathon conversations and noticing marathon advertisements.

Coincidentally, a friend asked her if she would like to join a 5km (3 mile) running clinic at the Running Room, the same organization where Karla started. Karen linked her newfound interest in marathons with the opportunity to join the Running Room. It was a good fit. The pie chart tool worked. What interested Karen became top of mind. She became more focused. The Running Room based their training on a cycle of "hard work, reward, rest," confirming her mother's words that if you work hard, you will see a positive return on investment. It became fused in her mind, and Karen now considers hard work to be one of her greatest assets.

Organizers rewarded everyone who finished or took part in something with a finisher's medal for their effort. The medals represented a tangible confirmation of the satisfaction of having completed a goal. They made Karen stop to reflect on her accomplishment. She felt good about what she had done. In Karen's words, "You plan for a 5km run, train several weeks for the 5km, run the 5km, and receive a medal for your efforts from a volunteer at the finish line who says congratulations. You are left with no choice but to stop in that moment and say, 'Yes, I did it'."

I asked Karen whether there would be a sense of loss when she completes the next race, and she said there is no last race or challenge. Life is a challenge; the work never stops. If life doesn't throw challenges her way, she will set one for herself and conquer it. She will add to and complete each section of her life pie chart. The sense of achievement and learning from a completed challenge motivates her to move on to the next one.

We can't all be Karen Meades, but her accomplishments can inspire us to just keep climbing towards our own goals and ambitions.

CHAPTER TEN

RUNNING THE ATACAMA CROSSING

The challenge faced by Karen Meades in any of her races must have been daunting. Most of us will never have the opportunity or desire to undertake what she has done, but her accomplishments are there for all of us to draw on, so we can keep climbing over any obstacles we may face.

In 2013, Karen raced through Chile in a challenge called the Atacama Crossing. Per their website, the Atacama Crossing is "a multi-stage ultramarathon that is known for its challenging terrain and harsh conditions, and it attracts runners from around the world who are looking for a unique and challenging endurance event. The Atacama Crossing is a self-supported race, so runners must carry all their own food, water, and equipment. The race covers approximately 250 kilometers (155 miles) over seven days, and runners must navigate through a variety of terrain, including sand dunes, salt flats, and rocky trails."

Karen was kind enough to share her personal notes from the run, offering a real-time glimpse into her motivation to "just keep climbing."

We arrive in San Pedro de Atacama in the wee hours of the morning—no problem—2-3 hours sleep, and I am on a bus to the start of the race; good times!!!

The Atacama was a huge challenge in so many ways—it was a mental game to push forward with a challenge… without my father—he passed away July 23. My relationship with my father was a very interesting one. He did one thing that I give him absolute credit for—he pushed me to face my challenges in life head on! I thought of him every day in the Atacama—it was a vast wilderness—I felt very small and very alone… I miss my father profoundly. I will never replace him in my heart or in my soul. I love my father!

The Atacama was a wonderful physical challenge—Day 1 started with a bang! 10,000 feet elevation—to explain the physical effect of altitude, you need only imagine running and breathing through a straw. It doesn't take long to feel dizzy, nauseous, that sort of flu feeling. The mind is amazing—in a way you know the physical symptoms you are feeling are not really the flu, but altitude; so somehow knowing this makes it possible to continue. I moved a little slower through this day trying to minimize the dizziness—feeling dizzy is unsettling. We were heading downhill over the course of the day, but during the day there were many uphill and downhills. It was a really tough day—I ended the day feeling that very familiar exhausted feeling. It's weird but I love that feeling—it reminds me of when I was a kid and I would play outside all day with my friends, discovering something or building something, and by the time I got back home I was simply exhausted! Anyway—back to the

Atacama.... So, Day 1 is over—I can't blog since I don't have my reading glasses and the computers are really tiny—yup welcome to being 50!!! Well, really, I'm 49... But it was a long day.

After you pass through the four checkpoints—where they provide you with water—that is all!!!!--you end the day at a base camp; Racing the Planet (race organizers) provides tents you share with 10 other people... Sam, a British journalist I met at the airport who works in Qatar for Aljazeera, is in my tent as well as one other British guy-Sam hates him from the word "hello." This is going to go well.... another British guy and five South Koreans—I'm trying to remember if South Koreans are the good ones, or the bad ones—I ask Sam (as it turns out they're the good ones).

So, Sam and Steve start at each other almost right away—apparently Steve's English isn't very good—sounds weird to me since all three of the Brits sound exactly the same—like the Queen—but they think Steve is a country bumpkin... You say tomato, I say tomato!

So, I pick a corner next to a South Korean, sleep with one eye open—still not sure about the whole Korean thing!

Flash forward to the end of the story—Sam and Steve have regular daily yelling matches, with swear words and everything—wish I have a video camera!!! Too funny!!! And the South Koreans are delightful—very nice eastern, modest, tranquil, family-oriented demeanor—one of the South Koreans goes to school at Cornell in the States and speaks English fluently. It was lovely chatting with them. We had a schoolteacher, a mathematician, a doctor, an elite Korean ultra-marathoner, and a South Korean marine with us—I told them I am an accountant—yup-a real conversation stopper! Let me add the night sky is spectacular—I have never seen so many stars—you can see the milky way!!!! You can see the milky way!!!!

So... Day 2—I'm feeling alive! Well, more like rusty!! So, Day 2 is harder than Day 1—how do they do that?! Day 2 starts with a descent into the Atacama slot canyon. The climbing is nuts. I'm afraid of heights—really afraid—and there is scary climbing. Ohhhh my Gosh!!!! Once down we cross the river—it is a river from the mountain glaciers, a freezing cold river. We crossed it multiple times over four or five hours, climbing up, then down, then crossing, then up, then down, then crossing—you get the idea. I can't believe it— flamingos (white ones), lizards (brown, green, blue ones), spiders, all living near the water. My feet and calves are numb... it is 50 degrees (yup 50 degrees—122 degrees Fahrenheit) feels like we are in the oven with our legs in a freezer... oh ya, and did I mention there is no air... I'm still sucking through a straw... and you ask me "why do I do this?" I bet you know the answer now!!!! So beautiful—so torturous.

Today, I meet the other Canadian at base camp—Jim—a colon cancer survivor—he really inspired me! Doctors had just informed him his cancer has returned and scheduled him for chemo—he takes a small break before starting the chemo to head out to the Atacama Desert—I'm thinking about Jim and cancer and the meaning of life as I am looking at the stars in the sky (half listening to Sam and Steve fight—you say tomato, I say tomato) as I fall asleep... I know why I do this!!!! I know!!!

Day 3–harder still—what is with these people? We must do an extra 14 kilometres (8 miles) because of the flash floods that hit Atacama this year—ok!! It is really cold in the morning—the winds come down from the mountains about 3am—it is so cold and so windy I wake up at 3am... the sleeping bag I have just isn't warm enough—I have no extra clothes to throw on and I can't close the "window." I am outside on the ground with a sleeping bag and my running clothes—I don't bring any change of clothes because it would be too heavy to carry, so I shiver... builds character I think I heard someone say!! Day 3 is called "crud" — that is really what they call it... A mixture of salt crust and dried mud—it looks like a field with grass, dry parched grass. It is a very hard packed ground, uneven, edgy with tufts of grass that is like wood it is so hard... the edges cut the bottom of my running shoes and tear my gaiters (the material glued to the top of my running shoe to keep the sand out). My father had always made my gaiters—this race is the first time I made them—they are holding up!! My boyfriend Nick (I call him Cracker) helped me—he rocks!!! As you are running, some of the crud holds you—some of it caves and you drop 3 maybe 4 inches. My ankles are aching... bruise on the bottom of my foot; shins are all cut up.

Our base camp is at the Licancabur Volcano!!! Wow—the scenery is unbelievable—I tried to notice as many details as I could—trying to take a picture to hold and to keep in my mind—I am so lucky!!! I am so grateful!!!

Day 4—the infamous salt flats-at the race debrief at 7:30 in the morning—The instructor tells us with the 8 years the Atacama race has been ongoing, competitors have pounded down the salt and created a trail—astronauts can now see the trail through the salt flats from space—cool! The salt flats are about 15 kilometres (9 miles) of the day, but they come with dire warning—do not enter the salt flats if you do not feel confident you can make it out! Ya, that's what they say—do not enter the salt flats if you do not feel you can make it out—the race organizers say it is very difficult if not impossible to come and get you in the salt flats... gulp... ok... so I am thinking we must go through the salt flats first in the day when we are "fresh" or as fresh as you can be on Day 4. Nope—we have some 10 or 15 km (six — nine miles) to do before the salt flats... gulp, gulp. I'm not afraid... ok well maybe very afraid... well, terrified is probably a better word... and I wanted to do this why??? Where are those encouraging emails???? I need to re-read them... brave, adventurous... I'm thinking small... little... scared.... accountant from Ottawa, Canada....... well... the salt flats came and went—I crossed with Sam (Aljazeera Sam) and we were ok—it was hot and the salt flats are a very unusual terrain, a crust on the top of soft brown sandy earth—so you break the crust and fall into the soft earth/dirt/sand... hard on the ankles and the bottom of your feet (sound familiar?)--really breathtaking when you are about half way in though—I am only one of a few thousand human beings who have been in the middle of the salt flats—now they are part of the earth that is protected and the only people who enter are the Atacama race participants... it is a very protected area.... But... You know the most amazing thing about Day 4? As I am coming to the last 2 kilometres (1 mile) of the day... I run into some tourists—I see the tourist bus and I see folks taking pictures of the Tebinquinche Lagoon—they call them the eyes—since the lagoon is in two parts—two eyes if you are looking from the sky... and one of the tourists is Cracker—ya. Cracker—serendipity!!!!! How does that happen—I scream, almost run him over as I run towards him—I am sooooo spicy, dirty, tired, wits end—run into his arms and I am happy, energized, laughing, motivated!!!!!! Wow, Cracker!!!!! He is on a tour—his tour lands him here at this time on this day—none of it planned-wow!!!!!! Serendipity—I am so happy!!! I love him so much!! We talk about what's left to the race—a long stage and a short village run, and we will meet at the finish line... I'm on the moon!!!

"The long stage—Day 5—comes and goes—I take 23 hours and 40 minutes—it was long but uneventful—I really can't say it was hard—other than being long—just long—longer than long—it was long. In the *middle of the night, all I want to do is curl up at the side of the trail and sleep. I start to fall asleep on my feet—then it feels like I am falling— then I wake up with an adrenaline rush—and the cycle repeats until daylight—when the sun rises it feels like I just woke up and I have this renewed energy—it is very interesting.*

The finish—16 kilometres (nine miles) on the last day—Sam and I finished in an hour and 20 minutes—-we ran together—the run is through the lovely village of San Pedro de Atacama—people are cheering along the route—Cracker is at the finish line—right on the line—I saw him right away!!!!

What an adventure!!!!! What an incredible adventure!!!!

CHALLENGED BY THE CHOICES WE MAKE

CHAPTER ELEVEN

CONSEQUENCES

The zig-zag path facing us as we make our way through life is littered with obstacles like a strategy game where our opponent tosses roadblocks in front of us every step of the way. Like a game, we have the same number of opportunities to screw it up as there are obstacles. And sometimes we do.

Except, what we are doing is not a game. The choices we make throughout our life determines our immediate future and, potentially, the eventual outcome. Sometimes, we have no option left but to go back to the beginning and start over or take a different path all together.

On January 16, 2009, Chris and I, along with fellow climber, Peter Yates, sat forcing down a sandwich at Stella Point. We rested with our backs against large, jagged boulders, nestled away from the chill blowing off glistening Rebmann Glacier a few feet away. We didn't say a word, saving our energy to breathe. One of our guides borrowed a camera from one of us to take a picture, so we each managed a weak smile.

A choice had to be made. This was the last rest stop before the push to the top. This would determine whether we would attempt to reach the summit and decide whether we would meet the goal that we had been working toward for months.

The first decision was our guides to make. The options were to continue climbing to the summit, veer off to Crater Camp, which didn't require higher altitude, or turn around and start back down. They'd been assessing our health throughout the climb with twice daily medical tests and questions they'd ask us along the way. Unbeknownst to us at the time, the guides designed the questions, which sometimes seemed to be out of left field, to assess our mental acuity. As we sat at Stella Point, we didn't realize the assessments had already been completed. The guides remained silent, other than perhaps a joke or two. No more questions. They had made their decision before we even arrived at this location.

We also had a choice. The options were the same as those considered by the guides. It turned out Chris had a severe headache brought on by altitude sickness that only the guides knew about. Peter seemed to be none the worse for wear, other than the shortness of breath affecting all of us and the torn ligament in his calf that had bothered him all the way up. A pressure, like a tight band, closed around my head, but not enough to even consider doing anything but continuing. By this point, I think I was operating in a fog anyway, but ready to complete the climb. We made the choice with no one saying a word.

It turned out to be the right choice. We were fortunate enough to have guides help us decide. Their silence spoke volumes. If they had thought we were in any danger, they would have spoken up and forced us to choose one of the other options or decided for us.

It's rare that we are fortunate to have guides who will point us in the right direction. In fact, sometimes it's just the opposite. Sometimes, people will guide us down the wrong path. Choices have consequences, and the last thing we want to do is to be overcome with regret after deciding. I had resolved to be satisfied with the outcome no matter what. I just had to be sure I had given it all the effort I could muster. Regret can debilitate and is to be avoided at all costs. It means we're living in the past, not looking forward. When we make a choice, it's done. If it turns out to be the wrong one, we face the consequences and make another choice. That is, to learn from the first choice we made and live with it, correct it, or let it eat us alive.

Without realizing, we make hundreds of choices every day. Some are as mundane as the channel to pick on TV or what to wear. I suppose they could become significant, and even overwhelming if we allowed them to, but in the overall scheme of things, they shouldn't amount to much. We subconsciously make plans and carry them out. Sometimes, they don't go so well. Something interrupts the plans we so meticulously laid out. It can be something we should have seen coming or it can be something completely unexpected that hits us like a punch in the mouth.

I'm sure the next two gentlemen who shared their stories had plans when they were growing up, but each got waylaid somewhere along the way. In effect, they got punched in the mouth, but they absorbed the punch and kept climbing. They made bad choices, but they faced the consequences and found the strength and support to correct their mistakes. There aren't enough adjectives to describe the strength required for them to realize their mistakes and the perseverance necessary to correct them. Many wouldn't have the same strength, support, and dedication to do what they did, and these two men are to be commended. They climbed over their mountains, and they're still climbing. Their accomplishments are tremendously inspirational.

I became aware of Daniel Crépault and Brian H. Singh through annual donations my wife and I make to a local drug treatment center called Harvest House. The center undertakes a fundraising activity each fall by selling calendars for the following year, and they do so by having one of their residents make a phone call to prospective donors to describe what the center has done for them. When I contacted Harvest House to see if someone would share their story, Daniel and Brian readily volunteered. Their stories unfold in the following chapters.

CHAPTER TWELVE

THE LIFE RECLAIMER
– PART 1

Dan Crépault grew up in a middle-class family. His father was a pastor, so Dan and his siblings spent a lot of time going to church when they were growing up. He started smoking cigarettes around age twelve, and soon after, began smoking marijuana and drinking alcohol. He thinks there were two reasons for going down that path. One was a desire to rebel against being a pastor's kid and the expectations that went with that label. Another part was needing to feel like he fit in, that he was accepted and admired by his classmates. Over the next five years (from twelve to seventeen), his life gradually fell apart as addiction made it increasingly unmanageable.

The major and most obvious challenge he faced in his youth was addiction. He could not cope with daily life without using either marijuana, alcohol, or prescription pills, or a combination of the three. The consequences of five years of substance abuse also created other challenges. These included dropping out of high school, criminal charges for property mischief, a damaged relationship with his parents, lost reputation, self-respect, self-esteem, motivation, self-awareness, etc. He had no money or employment, and by the end, he lost shelter when his parents kicked him out, the result of the five years of theft, lies, and abuse they had endured.

Dan faced other challenges that he wouldn't realize until years later. These were the core emotional and psychological problems and character defects that underpinned his addiction issues. They included problems with depression, explosive anger, tremendous insecurity, and crippling anxiety.

Dan has trouble pinpointing a defining moment where everything clicked in his head that he needed help. It was more of a gradual process where different realizations about himself and his situation coalesced. Finally understanding his problem needed to be addressed, Dan attended a one-year, residential addiction program at a treatment center called Harvest House Ministries in Ottawa, Canada. Three Christian businessmen founded Harvest House as an eight-bed residence in 1979, and in 1980, it moved to a more rural setting to house twenty-four residents. The rural setting removed the temptation of residents to return to the street. In 1985, they started a re-entry program to support residents in their drive to become functioning members of society. In 1992, Harvest House formalized a skills development program.

Dan was fortunate in that the treatment center took him right away with no waiting and without having to pay anything. He says this is not the case for many other programs. There can be long waiting lists and exorbitant costs associated with treatment. The treatment center charged him a minimal amount for rent and helped him apply for a government grant to cover it while he attended the center. He paid nothing out of pocket for his treatment.

During his first year, Dan received counseling and attended addiction education classes and recovery groups that helped him learn about his addiction and how to put it in remission daily. He also received help to upgrade his skills, building a resumé, and getting an education by earning a high school equivalency.

After completing the one-year program, he remained at the treatment center and took part in an additional year of after-care. During that year, he built on the recovery skills they had taught him, and opportunities arose to receive more experience. He increased his employability by volunteering at the center. He also took part in counseling focused on helping him identify and overcome the underlying problems that led him into addiction. This started an ongoing process of recovery from the previously identified challenges that continue to this day.

It took a few weeks after arriving at the treatment center before Dan understood he needed help. His parents offered to drive him to the center, and he agreed for lack of a better plan. Still unconvinced he needed help, even after enrolling in the treatment program, he still thought he was okay and a victim of circumstances. Arriving at the center arrogant, he thought he knew better than the people who wanted to help him, even though his experiences clarified he could not govern his own life successfully.

He was seventeen and felt out of place at the center because most of the guys in the program were so much older than him.

The drugs of choice for most were harder than the ones Dan used. They were using crack cocaine and methamphetamines, and some of the men came from jail or the street.

But Dan had a moment of clarity when he heard them speak about their experiences with addiction. Something clicked. He recognized he was on the same road as them, and the only difference was that they'd been traveling on that road longer. The gradual realization that he had the same core addiction problem as all the other guys led to another realization—that he would experience the same problems, such as homelessness, incarceration, deteriorating health, loss of employment, loss of family, premature death, etc., unless he followed the program. The realization scared him. It was a desperate and visceral fear. It motivated him to stay in the program, to listen to the staff, and to try to do what he was told. Even though there were challenges, he chose to just keep climbing.

He needed to know that the experts' advice on recovery from addiction made sense to him before he implemented it in his life. He needed mentors and coaches in recovery to gently, and sometimes not so gently, remind him that *his* best thinking put him in the mess he'd made of his life and that he should listen to people who knew more than he did and were qualified to guide him toward success. Prayer was a major way to deal with his problems as well. It was a constant source of help, strength, and guidance when he needed it most.

Dan points out that there are many barriers to accessing treatment. One factor is limited availability. There aren't nearly enough residential treatment programs to meet the demand. Then there are the wait times. He identified a statistic he had heard that the average wait time to access a publicly funded treatment resource in the province of Ontario, Canada is forty-two days. A lot can happen in the life of an addict, he said, if it is even close to that number, including changing your mind, missing your turn in the queue for a variety of reasons, or even overdosing. Many applicants are sitting in jail at the time they are called for treatment, and they need to be released by a judge, so they must wait for court dates, and that further affects their wait times. During that time, they are at greatest risk of changing their minds, relapsing, overdosing, and even dying.

Dan admits treatment wouldn't have been affordable if he'd had to pay for it. And if he'd had to wait months for a bed to become available, he may have changed his mind and decided not to enter the program by the time his turn came. In either of those cases, he says his ability to access treatment would have been seriously hampered and his life would have been drastically different today. He admits that he could have ended up dead, in jail, or severely damaged emotionally, psychologically, and physically, like so many others.

Today, Dan's been sober from drugs and alcohol for over eighteen years. He has a great relationship with his family, and his parents are proud of him. He has a family of his own with a beautiful wife and a sixteen-month-old son. Dan now works at the treatment center as the program director. The position gives him the responsibility and privilege to help the men who seek help for their addictions. In short, his life has changed completely.

When I asked Dan if he ever thought of giving up, his response was short and to the point. He said, "Regularly." He used education as an example. He arrived at Harvest House with two high school credits and no hope of graduating from high school. When he initially took part in the high school equivalency program the treatment center offered, he experienced a lot of tunnel vision. He couldn't imagine a future where he would be anything other than a high school dropout. The result was that he felt like giving up regularly. Mentoring and encouragement by others who had succeeded inspired him.

When he received his diploma, he saw they were right and that he could overcome challenges and be successful too. But the tunnel vision remained a problem with each new challenge that arose. For example, it came back again when he was finishing his doctoral dissertation. Stuck on the second chapter, his supervisor kept having him rewrite it because the direction was wrong. At that point, he experienced tunnel vision again, and he feared he would never finish his doctorate, even though he had already earned two degrees by that point. His mentor/pastor/sponsor encouraged him to continue to push onward, not to give up, and to have faith that everything would work out in the end. He finished the dissertation, defended it successfully, and earned the doctorate.

Still, Dan must keep climbing every day. He still feels like he has lots of problems. He has not arrived at a point in his recovery where everything is okay and he no longer needs to keep working on improving himself. Now, some of the greatest challenges he faces are the core underlying problems mentioned earlier, like depression, anger, insecurity, anxiety, and so on. The process for dealing with them is the same as what helped him deal with the other challenges he's faced.

For inspiration, he finds people he trusts who faced their issues successfully, and he follows their direction to the best of his abilities. As time went on in his recovery process, the mentoring or coaching relationships expanded to include other areas of his life, like employment, education, and dealing with relationships.

The last words go to Dan.

I learned that one secret to success is to find someone you trust, ask them what to do, and do what you are told. Doing it in different areas of my life allowed me to draw on the knowledge and experience of others. This was responsible for my successes, but it is also what kept me from giving up because those same coaches could reassure me that my struggles were normal and encourage me to keep going and not give up. The answer to my struggles is always the same, to keep putting one foot in front of the other, keep moving things forward, and having faith that the process (whatever process it is, whether it's the recovery process or the writing process, for example) will produce results.

CHAPTER THIRTEEN

THE LIFE RECLAIMER
– PART 2

Brian Singh was born in North York, Ontario, Canada, but grew up mainly in Brampton, Ontario. His parents immigrated from South America and always struggled with low income, but they worked hard to put a roof over the family's heads and food on the table. Brian's father was a good man, but when he drank, he became quite abusive towards him, his mother, and his older sister. His parents were very strict and did not let him do what other kids did. He always felt like his older sister was the golden child that his family cared more for and that he was just a mistake. Struggling with not fitting in with the others and not really having any friends, he kept to himself a lot, never feeling happy in life nor wanted. As a result, Brian became anxious and struggled with depression and suicidal thoughts. He never really understood the point of life. His parents didn't understand his emotions and feelings. Brian and his father often butted heads, never really saw eye-to-eye, and argued and fought regularly.

Brian reacted to the challenges he faced by rebelling as a teenager and young adult. He snuck out of the house and partied… a lot. He tried to impress people by being someone he wasn't and succumbed to peer pressure easily. His downfall started with stealing, which he considers his first addiction. He wanted the things everyone else had, things his parents couldn't provide. He would steal alcohol and cigarettes from his dad and take them to school, as well. That lead him to trying marijuana. Once he started partying, he dabbled in other drugs like ecstasy and cocaine.

He started using marijuana and alcohol regularly. It numbed the internal pain that he was going through in his brain. He tried seeking help from doctors for his depression. They prescribed different mood stabilizers and antidepressants, but none worked. It seemed like the only way he could numb the pain was with illicit drugs and alcohol. Over the next ten years, his drugs of choice were alcohol, marijuana, crack cocaine, and opioids—mixed for stronger results. He used for days on end sometimes. He worked to support his habit but never held down a job, so he also committed thefts and fraud to get his drugs. It often landed him in trouble with the law and, eventually, in jail several times. He tried moving to Alberta to get away from everything and everyone, hoping he might do better. It didn't help as he became homeless, living in his car in a Walmart parking lot for almost a year. He began smoking crack and heroin together and overdosed a few times, which landed him in the hospital. He hated himself, and his dark thoughts became so bad that he attempted suicide more than once.

Brian kind of knew early on that he needed help, but he didn't want to commit to it. He sought treatment in his early twenties, and he thought if it didn't work, then nothing would be different in his thirties. Fortunately, as much as he hated the world and wanted to kill himself, a small part of him wanted to live and lead a good life.

The moment of clarity that changed Brian's life came at the time of his last arrest. He swerved his car down the highway after three days of consecutive drug and alcohol use. He was on a mission to get more drugs, and he didn't care who he hurt on the way. It didn't matter if he killed himself or anyone else. He wanted more drugs. The police finally pulled him over, and as they arrested him, Brian told the officer that he didn't want to live anymore. They took him to the police station and then to the hospital. He attempted suicide again in the mental health unit, but security and nurses restrained him.

Brian spent about a month and a half in the mental health unit. He began to sober up and think clearly again. The doctors and psychiatrists worked with him to find a proper mixture and dosage of medications. Eating healthy and working out became part of his routine. He started reaching out to his family and pastor and opened up in group meetings. He decided in the hospital that he wanted to live and stop using drugs, and that he needed help to do it.

It wasn't just the hospital stay that convinced Brian he needed help. He needed inspiration, and he credits a few people for providing it. His mother and sister motivated him to seek treatment. They had been praying for him for years. He also talked to his pastor. He credits the psychiatrist, a Christian lady who told him about Harvest House, the same treatment center that Dan Crépault went to. She convinced him there was so much more to life, and he understood that he could have a brilliant future. While in the mental health unit, he met many people who struggled with addiction and were hurting just like him. He realized he wasn't the only one. The last penny dropped when the hospital discharged a man from the same unit as Brian. Two days later, word got back that he had overdosed and died. That's when Brian decided he needed to commit to his sobriety. The image of meeting the man's parents and watching them laugh together during their visit convinced Brian he didn't want to put his family through that.

But his challenges had just begun. Once he began looking at treatment centers, he discovered getting in was easier said than done. A lot of them were quite expensive, and even though his family agreed to help, they couldn't afford the cost. Also, the pandemic was raging, and most treatment centers had cut occupancy limits in half, so waitlists were long. Distance also remained an issue. Some treatment centers resided in other provinces. The biggest issue was his suicidal history. Treatment centers were not willing to take him as they considered him a liability. He dealt with the issues with persistence and prayer! Even though Harvest House initially denied him, he called back, begged, and told them he wanted to live and get sober and that he was desperate for help. They finally agreed.

Brian thought of quitting many times. Recovery is not a straightforward thing. It would have been so much easier to just give up and die. Desperation and determination pulled him through. He discovered the fight is never over. Every day is a constant battle. Addiction and recovery never take a break. Every morning, when he wakes up, he asks God for the strength not to give up. Sometimes, he still thinks about going back to the drug life. It just seems to him to be so much easier than real life. However, that is his addict mind at work, and he reminds himself of the pain he went through.

The stories told by others in the treatment center inspired Brian, seeing them with thirty-plus years of sobriety and where they are now. He knew that if he could get through this, he could accomplish anything in life. Living with twenty other addicts, people just like him, helped. He wasn't the only one feeling that way, and he had people with him on his journey through recovery. He had seen many friends leave and end up either dead or in jail, and he knew if he left, that's what waited for him.

Brian sees a different pandemic than the rest of us. He sees a pandemic of drug addiction and alcoholism. Wherever he goes, he will always be in the presence of these substances. When put in these situations, he says he needs to remember the things he learned in recovery. He knows he will go through trials and tribulations in life. He knows there will be hard times and stresses of life ahead. Challenges to face. Mountains to climb. However, he will use the tools handed to him to get through. He will just keep climbing.

The last words go to Brian.

My life has changed more than I ever thought it would. I have a totally new outlook on life. I love the man I see in the mirror these days, and my family and I are closer than we've ever been, even my father. I see a great future for myself, and I've developed a passion for wanting to help people just like me.

CHALLENGES
NO ONE
ASKED FOR

CHAPTER FOURTEEN

CHALLENGE VERSUS ADVERSITY

If ever there was a word in the English language that is overused in my humble opinion, it's adversity. A hockey player faces adversity because he or she has an ankle sprain. A football team is facing adversity because they are losing by a touchdown, it's fourth down with eight yards to go, and a few seconds left on the clock. Or a baseball team faces adversity when it's down three games to none in a seven-game series. A soldier faces adversity while he huddles in the pouring rain in a trench, his bloodshot eyes widening with fear as the enemy zeros in on his location and the thump of grenades and the whine of bullets grows louder.

Wait! What!?

The same word is used to describe an athlete with a physical problem, a team facing a loss or being eliminated from the playoffs, and a soldier whose life is being threatened! Merriam Webster defines adversity as "a state or instance of serious or continued difficulty or misfortune," while a challenge is a "stimulating task or problem." Technically, the term adversity applies to the athlete and the teams, but there seems to be a disconnect. I'm not about to argue with Merriam Webster, but surely, the stronger word, which I prefer to think adversity is, should be reserved for situations like the one the soldier is in. I admit the words "problem" and "challenge" aren't as sexy and wouldn't sell newspapers, but for this book, I'll reserve adversity for the type of challenge no one asks for.

Imagine you're driving a tractor trailer through the mountains, something most of us will never experience. You've driven up the winding highway with your freight-ladened 18-wheeler and reached the crest. The slow drive seemed to take forever as the engine labored with the heavy load. The brilliant afternoon sun glints off the hood ornament you polished that morning, you have your sunglasses on, and classic rock fills the cab from satellite radio. Experience on this highway reminds you that the longest, steepest drive on the route awaits on the other side of the crest. You recall your apprehension on this slope as a rookie driver, but today is just another day on the road. Smoke puffs from the twin stacks behind the cab as you shift down to slow the vehicle and start down the slope. A car is a hundred yards ahead, so you back off to provide more separation.

You start the descent toward the lush valley. Tapping the brakes comforts you as the huge vehicle's eighteen wheels respond. Every brake in the system will be required on this ride into the valley. In an ideal world, the truck would have Jake brakes, which use compressed air in the engine to slow the rig. They're so much better on a drive like this since simply removing your foot from the pedal engages the system. But that loud rump-rump-rump sound as the truck slows is too much for some latte-drinking suburban dwellers, so local authorities proclaimed them illegal in some neighborhoods. Today, your rig only has a standard braking system to slow the eighteen wheels and the considerable weight of the vehicle. It's a big ask of the braking system on the slope you're starting down.

You're riding the brake hard because of the steepness of the slope, and about halfway down, the pedal seems to depress more than normal. A jolt of adrenaline snakes up your spine. It can only mean one thing. Your heart rate speeds up and dampness forms in your armpits as another step on the brake does nothing. You no longer hear the music blasting from the radio as you're focused on what is happening. The heavy truck is picking up speed, rapidly closing the distance on the car in front. You can see the heads of two kids in the back. You're thankful you backed off, providing some distance between your truck and the car, but the gap is closing too fast.

Blurred rocks and trees speed past the side window in your peripheral vision. Slow, deep breaths through your mouth help to slow your heart rate as this trip that should have been routine has turned into adversity. The truck is flying now. The enormous weight is threatening to push the heavy trailer sideways and forcing the entire rig forward at outrageous speed. Your knuckles are white on the steering wheel, trying to keep the truck on the road. Pumping the brakes just reinforces the fact you're facing a big problem. The gap between your truck and the car has narrowed to a few hundred feet, so you sound a blast of the air horn as a warning. You can see the kids laughing at something in the back seat, and the driver seems oblivious as your front bumper edges terrifyingly close to the rear of the car. Both vehicles are close to the bottom of the slope when you spot something just ahead. Something that could save your life and the lives of the people in the car.

It's a gravel-covered road connecting to the main highway and continuing up the other side. It's called a runaway escape ramp, or emergency ramp, among other names, and it's designed for this purpose. Should a truck's brakes overheat and fail on the downward slope of a mountainside, the roads offer an escape route or offramp for the driver to aim his truck at to slow it down. It's a lifesaver.

Like the truck driver with the option of the runaway escape ramp, most of us have a choice when faced with a challenge. Chris, Peter, and I had an offramp when we climbed the mountain. We could have turned around and come down at any time. One of our porters carried a portable hyperbaric chamber, stretcher, and oxygen if things got really bad. Every step of the way, we had an escape route. We may not have liked the escape route we would have been forced to take, but it was there for the taking. The same applies to most of the challenges we face. We decide to go one direction or another, and even if our original decision is bad, we usually have the option of fixing it or going in a different direction. Like the trucker, we must assess the situation, decide, and choose the next path.

Most of the people documented in this book had options if their chosen path did not turn out. Jen, Karla, and Karen gave themselves challenges, but they could have done something different had their challenges not worked out.

Sometimes, we give ourselves challenges that turn out badly, and the offramp is not so easy to take. Dan and Brian gave themselves challenges through choices that turned out badly. By persevering, they extracted themselves from their original choices and took an offramp to a better one.

Sometimes, our choices can lead to situations we don't ask for. A challenge can grow to become adversity. No matter what happens, we have to just keep climbing. An example is the story of the twelve-member junior football team and their coach who hiked into a cave in Thailand in 2018 only to have their way blocked by a torrential rainfall, which sealed off their escape route. The boys and their coach challenged themselves by exploring the cave, but their challenge turned into adversity when finding a way out seemed impossible.

The next two people are clearly facing adversity, at least according to my interpretation of the word. They have been handed challenges they didn't ask for and are rising to the occasion as best they can under the circumstances. Most of us can only imagine what they are going through. They are tremendously inspirational because of their determination to make the best of critical situations, their desire to be examples for others, and their will to keep climbing. For security reasons, it is essential to change one of their names.

I don't think it is a challenge to be inspired by Elisa Beth Magagna and Edwin.

CHAPTER FIFTEEN

THE POSITIVE PATIENT

Elisa Beth Magagna and I met through social media. I'm not sure who connected with whom first, but I remember Elisa's incredibly positive posts. They were humorous, heartfelt, detailed, and uplifting. In fact, if you read her posts, you would never realize the adversity she is facing. She's an extremely positive person, and I'm sure her family is exceptionally proud of her.

Elisa has stage four melanoma.

Elisa grew up at the mouth of Big Cottonwood Canyon, which is part of the Wasatch Mountain range in Utah. Her days involved climbing, skiing, and hiking as a kid, and something about being in the mountains, playing music and writing, really ignited a lifelong passion for her. She had played the violin and piano since kindergarten, as a preteen and then teenager, and just couldn't get enough of playing music in the mountains—sometimes for hours each day. She would even write stories, lyrics, and poems up on those beautiful trails.

Despite her passion for music and writing, Elisa had a difficult life growing up. She ended up running away from home at seventeen. She made the drastic decision to leave when her life took a shocking turn. Her local nondenominational church performed an exorcism on her. She now says she made a mistake, but it was one that countless others have done without repercussions. She wasn't married, but she had sex.

The self-righteous church leaders frowned upon this and claimed that, somehow, the devil was transferred to her during the act. It was enough to prompt the assistant pastor and others to perform the exorcism. It was a frightening and painful experience as they gathered around, shouting at her and laying their hands on her. Her faith took a hit that day. It would have been enough to discourage anyone. She tried to recover from the experience by playing her fiddle up the California coast before flying to Hawaii where she busked as a homeless street musician on the Waikiki Strip for several months.

Eventually, Elisa came home, married, and gave birth to her first baby at eighteen—talk about growing up fast. She loved her baby's first few months when she found out she was pregnant with a second baby! When she was only nineteen, Elisa's second child was born with birth defects. Born in November, he died the following January, which left a hole in her heart that would never fully heal.

While Elisa was about to face even bigger challenges, at nineteen years of age she had already lived a lifetime. She always coped with music, writing, and her faith in God. During her son's hospitalization, if she wasn't composing songs about life's trials, she would journal on anything available, such as napkins, the back of medical handouts, receipts…

you name it. But after her son's death, she didn't have the strength or courage to read her own words for several years, until she was twenty-six. A friend read what Elisa refers to as scribblings at one point and said they helped her so much. Despite being told by teachers in the past that she wasn't good at writing, Elisa tried to find a publisher for her book. She finally published her first book, *The Golden Sky*, in 2011 and has since sold over 36,000 copies of her books.

More trouble lay ahead for Elisa. In 2018, doctors diagnosed her with stage 2B melanoma on her left wrist—the one that holds her violin. They took over an inch of skin on each side and tissue deep down into the muscle and tendon. The doctors told her she might not play the violin again because that's the hand that plays notes on the strings. She admits she cried, so lost, and went to a local church, begging them to let her play at the altar the night before her surgery.

After the doctors performed the surgery and she'd spent months working on her wrist's functionality, she eventually retrained her fingers and wrist to play again. It felt like a small eternity, but Elisa thinks she plays even better now than she did before.

Doctors originally thought they'd removed all the cancer, but it became stage four in 2020. Tumors infiltrated every one of Elisa's vertebrae, she had two tumors in her brain, and growths appeared in her lungs. After seeing the extent of the progression, doctors gave Elisa the devastating news that she would only live two more years. Through it all, she's had many surgeries (the spinal team removed her entire L3 vertebra); brain, back, and pelvis radiation sessions, bone infusions, cancer treatments…

She remembers staring out the hospital window, so scared. But then, she thought she had two options: let the prognosis ruin the rest of her life or make the best of things. That's when she made a list of what *she* could control of what *she* wanted to do with the rest of her short life: get published after writing about her battle against cancer, visit Italy, go skydiving with her family, and somehow, share her story with other people who needed encouragement.

Elisa admits there have been many times when she felt like giving up. Her life had been so hard. She lost a child, divorced, and put herself through school as a single mom to get her bachelor's degree and better support her children. And then, to get remarried finally and receive a cancer diagnosis… It must have been almost unbearable.

She overcame the feelings by being joyful. She says that for her, true joy isn't like happiness. Happiness can come and go, but to Elisa, joy is synonymous with perseverance. She chooses to be joyful—to be grateful that she's still alive. That's really the best thing any of us can do with the time we have left.

I asked Elisa how she kept climbing through everything she has been through. I'll leave it to her to respond in her own words.

> *My love for God, my husband, and my kids keeps me going. But I think I just really enjoy life. I'm in pain most days, but I still look forward to the little miracles, like playing board games with my family or jamming on the fiddle when I feel up to it. I'm just so grateful to still be here, enjoying every second that I can. I would love to see my kids grow up more than anything, get their careers,*

and maybe even get married. But I'm just trying to live in the moment and enjoy every second of life that I can. We've checked almost everything off my bucket list, and that's been fun too. Italy was even more amazing than I'd ever hoped, and it shocked my oldest daughters that I went skydiving with them!

In typical Elisa fashion, she says, "I even lost my hair and some of my dignity!" Recently, when someone asked if she's in remission, she said, "No. But my shitty attitude sure is!"

I don't know if her attitude has ever been shitty, but if it has, no one could blame her after everything she's been through. Whenever everything is feeling overwhelming and the world seems to be a mess, I urge you to re-read the story of this brave woman. I don't think anyone could handle adversity any better than Elisa, but we can all aspire to do so. As she posted recently, "It's smart to face the facts and fight like hell."

You can read more of Elisa's journey on social media under the pen name EC Stilson. Readers can find her books on Amazon, including *Two More Years, The Golden Sky, Homeless in Hawaii, The Sword of Senack, A Stranger's Kindness,* and more.

CHAPTER SIXTEEN

THE RESOLUTE FAMILY

Edwin lives in a small village of about 3,000 people in Cameroon in central Africa. I have changed his name to protect his identity for reasons you will understand as you read his story. We met through social media during the time my wife and I were fundraising.

I recall one winter afternoon when I was busy in my office. I opened the blind during a lull in my writing and sat staring out the window, watching the snow cascade down. It was pretty, but snowing so much, it was impossible to do anything but sit inside waiting for the storm to subside. As my thoughts wandered and the snow piled up, my computer blipped with a message from Edwin. He was just checking in, as we do from time to time. We have stayed in touch since we first met online, so it was always enjoyable to receive a message from him.

If there's one thing that Canadians have a reputation for, other than saying sorry a lot, it's talking about the weather.

I complained about the cold and snow and how it was impossible to do much outside. I explained I would shovel later. When I finished complaining, Edwin told me how he couldn't imagine the cold and snow, having never experienced it. I asked how he was doing, and his answer shocked me. He said that he and his family were hiding in the bush from the military. A helicopter circled overhead.

I couldn't believe it! I had just spent five minutes of his time complaining about the weather while he faced adversity, worried about his safety and that of his family. Talk about putting things into perspective. It's a reminder of how fortunate we are to have been born in a safe country and how we can't imagine how others are feeling without walking in their shoes. The incident seared that memory into my brain. How embarrassing to have complained about such a trivial thing. His obvious strength that came across in that brief conversation inspired me. I wanted to hear more of Edwin's story and why he keeps climbing under the immense challenges he didn't ask for. This is his story.

Edwin's passion is agriculture, but things were never easy growing up with his family. He describes living in a rural setting in Cameroon as very challenging. There were no good seeds to plant, prices were low, the roads were poor, and access to health care was sometimes not available. Despite the challenges, relative peace existed in their area. People slept soundly at night and got up in the morning without fear. They moved about freely to meetings and events.

Everything changed in December 2018, when fighting started in Edwin's community.

To understand what Edwin and his family are going through now, it is necessary to reflect on the conflict. He explains that there were two Cameroons under the United Nations' trusteeship: British Southern Cameroon, which represented about 20% of the population (ruled by Britain) and French Cameroon, representing the other 80% of the population (ruled by France). French Cameroon received independence in 1960 and became known as the Republic of Cameroon. The United Nations voted fifteen votes to thirteen that British Southern Cameroon could become independent, but Britain refused to grant it, stating that the territory in question was not economically viable.

In 1961, Britain organized a plebiscite by which the people of Southern Cameroon could express their preference for one of two options to gain independence: join either Cameroon or Nigeria.

The people voted to join Cameroon in a federation, and officials developed a constitution which stated expressly that any modification tampering with the constitution's integrity would be null and void. In 1972, the then president organized a referendum against those tenets of the constitution. French-speaking citizens took part in a vote that did not concern them. In the end, the vote passed, and officials changed the name of the country from the Federal Republic to the United Republic of Cameroon.

A second president came to power and changed the name again to the Republic of Cameroon. This made matters worse as the new name was the same as that given to French Cameroon when they received their independence. People argued that the English part of the country had disappeared from the map.

The minority English-speaking population felt repressed by the French-speaking majority. Once considered one of Africa's most stable countries, Cameroon became a country divided by two different regions. Problems deepened when the government started deploying French teachers into English schools. They also deployed French justices and magistrates in common law courts, and the working language in all offices became French.

In 2016, The English-speaking minority rose as one. Lawyers, students, and teachers from the country's English-speaking minority launched protests objecting to their under-representation and cultural marginalization by the central government. But the government reacted violently, killing many people. The military used helicopter gunships to shoot directly at citizens. Many died because their families could not take them to the hospital at night for fear of attack. Sometimes, the military burned the food, or it rotted on the farm because farmers couldn't take it to market through the fighting. Sometimes, people stayed in their houses for weeks because of lockdowns. Freedom of movement became limited.

The government tried to use conciliatory measures, but the long-simmering unrest grew when some separatist leaders symbolically declared independence for two English-speaking regions. Skirmishes continued with accusations of brutality on both sides.

Edwin saw the effects of tear gas for the first time in 1990. One person was killed, but it was nothing like December 2018, when the military swept through the village, killing any man they met and burning houses as they went. One day in his village, they killed seven people and razed twenty-five homes. The elderly, the mentally deranged, babies, and young men and women lost their lives.

Edwin describes the effect on him and his family.

That fateful day in December, we woke to the sound of heavy gunshots. Taken unawares, confused at hearing a gun for the first time, it appeared like the world was ending. When the military came, people escaped to bushes and other nearby villages. I grabbed my one-year-old son and, together with my wife and two siblings, we alighted out of the house. Behind us, we could hear gunshots and explosions and then saw smoke billowing from houses. It was a dark Saturday. Multitudes of people strung the road; kids carrying bags, mattresses, and buckets while the older struggled to keep pace. As we moved on, deserted homes stared at us, as if we were in the spirit world. The owners of these homes had fled before we got there. I trekked with my family to a nearby settlement about three kilometers away from our home, and we were there for two days. Some people moved permanently. When we returned, the military came in again, and this time, I sent my wife, son, and my two siblings to meet my sister in another remote village twenty-five kilometers away. I had to remove everything from my house to a safe location. I was alone in the house for about three months until the military incursions started reducing. Once convinced that the military had returned to the barracks, we could safely return to our homes. Sadly, the military would break into houses and hide, killing the first people that returned home. It was a once-in-a-lifetime, horrifying experience. Now, when my five-year-old son hears gunshots, he asks whether the military is coming.

No child should have to ask that question, and no parent should have to answer it. Edwin hears names of guns from his son: AK (submachine gun), G3 (automatic weapon), Bira (mechanical machine gun), etc. As Edwin so succinctly describes his sentiments, "It's just sad."

Years later, the conflict continues to rage, yet Edwin and his family are still in the same community. In his community of 3,000, fifty-four people have died because of the conflict and related causes. In its May 9, 2022 report, the Foreign Policy Research Institute wrote, "*The international community has fallen asleep at the wheel when it comes to the crisis in Cameroon. Brutal killings, burned villages, and hundreds of thousands of displaced people—and the reaction is a deafening silence.*"

Edwin explained that Southern Cameroon comprises two provinces, twelve divisions, with a population of about eight million people. All these divisions are fighting for their independence. To escape from this conflict, one must travel either to Nigeria or cross over to the French-speaking part of Cameroon. Some people traveled to other countries, including members of the military who do not want to fight. Edwin could have moved, but he wanted to stay.

When asked why he kept climbing by staying in his small village, he answered:

> There is no greater thing one can be in this world than to be remembered for what he has done for his people and the world. If I got killed during this war, I'd have died like a hero, and people would remember me for that, though that was not my intention. I just wanted to stay with my family and the rest of the people who didn't want to leave.
>
> I want the people who will be here in the next twenty, forty, sixty, one hundred years to know that there was somebody like me. I come from one of the poorest families here, and I could not have completed primary school if not for one of my teachers, who noticed that I was no longer coming to school. Being exceptionally intelligent, she vowed to send me to wherever I wanted to go. Sadly, the teacher died when I was

still in secondary school. I studied up to the second year in university. It was extremely difficult to continue. Rent and food were expensive, and I was sleeping on a mat on a bare floor. My ill-health made it worse, and I had to withdraw. I was studying life sciences.

Thousands have fled to neighboring cities, but Edwin and his family are still there. When asked why, he offered several reasons.

1. *Not allowing oneself to be ruled by fear is the ultimate decision. People have overcome situations worse than this one, so why not me?*

2. *Once you're pushed to the wall, you'll have to push back; nowhere to go. You can't break the wall.*

3. *Trapped between the rock and the hard place, which is the case with us, there was no option than to stay until somebody comes and rescues us. To this day, we're still waiting for that person to come. We f l e e , first to the bush before thinking of the next move, and then comes the inevitable hunger. You look at your family, and there is not even water to drink. Many returned to get food and water, only to be killed.*

4. *Traveling is a nightmare. You must put together all the odds before embarking on a journey. The main urban center close to my community is about 110km (68 miles) away. Formerly, there used to be three checkpoints, but now there are fifteen. Three separatist checkpoints and twelve military. At some checkpoints, passengers are required to pay money to the military or separatists. A journey of two hours now takes eight hours through bush roads.*

5.   *You need courage to move from one area to another, even in your own locality.*

6.   *With the education of kids stalled for over six years and watching them grow to adults with empty heads, we had to look for alternative education methods. The solution became community schools and child friendly spaces set up by the United Nations International Children Emergency Fund (UNICEF) in countries where there is war to enable children to learn.*

Edwin has shown extraordinary human perseverance and determination, stretched to the limit, but still able to face the prevailing situation. His passion for agriculture suffers as he must watch as families are at risk of starvation in the shorter term. In the longer term, there is a need to increase food production and engage in community development projects to fight poverty, starvation, disease, and illiteracy.

There has been some improvement. The warring parties seem to recognize civilians now. The killing is no longer as rampant as it used to be. Some people are opening businesses, and farming activities are going on, though farmers are still paying a lot of money to separatists and the military. Development projects are happening, too.

Yet it's not over. We continue to live in fear, but fear cannot defeat us. We're used to the hardship, struggling to feed our families, find basic medical supplies, kids out of school for six years and counting. Presently, it's still difficult for children to study conveniently. Many are still caught in the crossfire and some schools cannot open their doors. Over three-quarters of pupils and students are out of school either in

Nigeria or in the French-speaking part of Cameroon. Many English schools are open now, but parents pay enormous sums to allow their children to study. Two of my siblings were in primary five and six when the war started, but now, they are so grown that they would no longer want to sit in class with kids. Their mates are already in high school. The challenges are enormous, and there is no end in sight.

It's hard to imagine what life must be like for Edwin and his family. When he and his family fall asleep at night and get up the next morning, they count themselves lucky. Many people have gone into hiding for fear of the unknown. It's a lawless society. Edwin's handling of the situation is truly inspirational. When handed adversity they didn't ask for, he and his family faced it head on. They kept climbing, and like everyone else in this book, they did so for their own reasons. They are role models for all of us. The challenges most of us will meet in our lives pale by comparison, so when it's figuratively snowing in your life, think of Edwin and his family hiding in the bush in Cameroon.

KEYS TO
JUST KEEP
CLIMBING

CHAPTER SEVENTEEN

AGE ISN'T A BARRIER

I'm sure Karen Meades would not even give it a second thought, but a 1,600 km (994 mile) run the entire length of the U.K. at age fifty-nine is a tremendous accomplishment. Gabriella Varga stepped on stage for the first time as a competitive bodybuilder at forty-five. Changing careers as Jen Gilroy did later in life requires courage and self-confidence, and Karla Del Grande just keeps running. Just as these strong women did, understanding that age isn't a barrier has gone a long way to help me just keep climbing. At the other end of the spectrum, is young Coltan Tanner, who climbed Mount Kilimanjaro at age six. I'll be focusing on my side of the age scale because I have difficulty relating to what he did, but remember, we can set goals and overcome challenges at any age.

I retired for the first time in 2004 at age fifty-five. I had no proper plans, other than to play golf and enjoy life, even though the experts advise that retirement is a major life change. They were right. It isn't something to go into blindly. They warn about pitfalls that can include boredom, disappointment, or even depression as retirees no longer have the daily support group of friends and acquaintances. People who managed staff during their working life no longer have that energizing feeling of guiding their group to meet a goal, and those who were staff no longer have the satisfaction of teamwork to complete a project. Sometimes, the so-called golden years may not be so golden. All the pre-retirement courses tell us that retirement requires pre-planning and discussions with your spouse about what it is going to look like. Of course, finances also come into the mix.

Working from home during the pandemic may prepare some for retirement. While the introverts among us may prefer the solitude of working at home, removing the social interaction of working at the office may not be a good thing. We all need friends throughout our lives to talk to and do things with. I'm fortunate that some people I worked with are friends to this day, and my wife and I have met new friends through church and other activities. It's good to see them again after the pandemic.

I enjoyed my career working for the Canadian federal government and because of that, it went by in the blink of an eye. I'm finding retirement is the same. Ask any retired person, and they'll tell you they are busier in retirement than when they worked. The time races by, and we need to pay attention. It's possible we feel busy during retirement because we do things a little slower. I know on a day I have nothing planned that I do things a little more leisurely, but the hours still seem to slip by. If time is passing quickly, it means you're enjoying the people in your orbit and what you're doing. We must savor the moments as they pass by.

The great thing about retirement is that we get to choose what we want to do, not what someone is telling us to do. But until we're ready, it may not be enough. Initially, I stayed retired for a few months. We enjoyed a holiday after retirement in April, and golf and work around the yard filled my days in the summer. But then winter arrived, and boredom set in. I took a short contract with a consulting firm and was back to being around people and contributing. Before long, I consulted more and more, and did so for the next ten years. I was fortunate to consult on my terms, working through the winter and never taking a contract through the summer months.

Just like my actual career, I look back fondly on my consulting days. New friends came into my life, and I considered each time I finished a contract to be another retirement. I lost track, but I "retired" about twelve times. I had my health scare during the time I consulted and started training for the Kilimanjaro climb. I realized that life is like a good meal. We know it's going to end sometime, so we have to savor every morsel.

Some questioned my sanity at wanting to climb a mountain at my age, but the thought never occurred to me, other than when they brought it up. The question for me was not my age. It was whether I could become fit enough to give myself a chance to succeed.

I'm sure it took longer to get in shape because I was older. Years of sitting behind a desk were against me. Just the sheer physiological changes from aging made it more challenging to prepare than if I had been, say, thirty years old,

LIFE IS LIKE A GOOD MEAL. WE KNOW IT'S GOING TO END SOMETIME, SO WE HAVE TO SAVOR EVERY MORSEL.

like our son, Chris. If I pulled a muscle, it took longer to heal than it would have if I was younger. But to all that, I say, "So what?" It was a challenge which I happily accepted.

The satisfaction of consulting ended one morning when I woke up and struggled to find the motivation to get up to go to work, even though it meant walking about twenty-five steps in my pajamas from the bedroom to my home office. The passion I had for my work was gone. It became obvious my consulting days were done, and it was time to focus on other things.

I try not to contemplate age, even though the reminders are constant. Something as simple as our grandkids looking at us blankly when we talk about the Beatles or Neil Armstrong's walk on the moon remind us. Or the knees that ache sometimes, or the doctor's appointments. It's not being able to dredge up a name until three o'clock in the morning. And, of course, mirrors don't lie. I'm always happy now when the grandkids comment on my gray hair because at least it's a reminder that I still have some, although it's disappearing at an alarming rate. None of these things should be a deterrent to enjoying every day to its fullest. It just means we must keep climbing.

As mentioned, the Kili climb led to many changes in my life, including an improvement in diet and exercise, but there were many other changes that occurred because of the trip as well. Meeting the children in a classroom we helped to fund from money donated to our cause gave me a sense of admiration and optimism. Admiration for the smiling, friendly Tanzanian kids in ragged clothes willingly attending classes when they could with barely any pencils, books, or paper. Optimism because I had time to do something about their plight. I was determined to do what I could, and over ten years, with the help of good friends, Evelyn and I raised money through variety shows and golf tournaments to complete four projects in Tanzania in conjunction with Plan International Canada and contribute to the service dog program for Wounded Warriors Canada.

Chris and I started doing presentations about the climb and realized there was a book waiting to be written about our story, so that led to *Kilimanjaro and Beyond: A Life-Changing Journey.* When I started connecting with other authors, I realized I was significantly older than most of them. I had had no formal training in creative writing. What I had was a life of experience, including writing financial policy for several years. One could say it was the school of hard knocks. Nobody reads financial policy unless their work requires them to do so, but I enjoyed the process, and it honed my writing skills. After publishing *Kilimanjaro and Beyond*, I wrote a travel memoir called *I Guess We Missed the Boat* about our adventures traveling with Evelyn's side of the family. My target audience was really the family, but it turned out to be popular among the older crowd, and it encouraged me to continue writing.

I challenged myself to write fiction. Accountants are not supposed to be creative. In fact, if they're too creative, they could end up in jail! Writing fiction was foreign to me, but I tried anyway. That led to a five-book thriller series, and I'm now working on the third book in a mystery series.

Writing led to yet another challenge. I had to learn something about marketing! I discovered that writing is only the tip of the iceberg. No one will read a book if they aren't aware it exists. The author knows what the book's about, why he or she wrote it, and the type of readers it would attract, so who better to market it, right? Well, it's not that simple. Like everything else, there's a learning curve, and the landscape changes daily with new promotion opportunities, evolving reader taste, and updated technology, such as artificial intelligence. New phrases, like line and developmental edits and traditional versus independent publishing, became part of my vocabulary, and suddenly, I was an entrepreneur navigating the book selling world.

The most exciting part of writing for me is the research required for each book. Different scenarios that arise in each story require significant research to ensure they are factually correct, even though most of my writing is fiction. It's a learning experience every day. Writing and everything that goes with it has become another exciting challenge to overcome after "retirement."

It's possible to do things we enjoy and undertake new challenges as we age. Of course, there are some things we may not do as well, or maybe some we can't do at all. We may have physical challenges that prevent us from undertaking activities we used to do easily. If that's the case, there's no choice but to accept our limitations and adjust our definition of success. It's difficult to accept sometimes, but I think we need to find something that will still challenge us to give our life meaning.

I took on another challenge at sixty-nine years of age when I started playing guitar. With the help of YouTube videos and encouragement and sage advice from our singer/songwriter son, Trevor, I've learned to play a few songs. Not well, but I can play them.

This is a good example of resetting our definition of success. Guitar doesn't come naturally to me. That's my excuse, anyway. It probably doesn't for anybody since becoming proficient requires years and thousands of hours of dedicated practice. I'm convinced that age makes it a little more difficult if one is just starting to play a musical instrument. Now, here comes my second excuse. With guitar, the fingers don't stretch as far as they need to sometimes and changing chords as quickly as required on some songs becomes a challenge. I will never be in a band or playing in public at all, but that's okay. Playing for half an hour or so every day makes me happy, so I do it.

An eighty-six-year-old golfer put things into perspective when we discussed our respective games one day. He doesn't hit the ball as far as he used to, but he said he has never played better. That makes little sense, doesn't it? But when he elaborated, it made perfect sense. He continued to tell me that even though he doesn't hit the ball as far, and he takes a couple of extra strokes to get down the fairway, he stays out of trouble, He's never in the trees. Never in the water. He uses the same ball for five or more games. He can still chip and putt. He's playing the same game, just differently. His story makes me look forward to playing golf at eighty-six so I can spend less money on balls and shoot a lower score! It's another example that we need to do what we enjoy, even if we do it slower, and savor every moment.

During the pandemic, I needed a way to get out into the fresh air and to stay active. Golf courses and gyms were closed. So, I signed up for virtual hikes online. By virtual hikes, I don't mean lying on the sofa dreaming of hiking. Certain websites offer the opportunity to count steps towards a goal, such as walking Hadrian's Wall in North England or Nova Scotia's Cabot Trail. It's encouragement to be active and see sites around the world without the expense of leaving your community. Most of the web sites offer the option to view your current location on your hike online, and they send electronic postcards at milestones along the journey and a medal at the end. At the time of writing, I'm working my way along the 3,513 kilometer (2,182 mile) Great Wall of China. It will take about three years to complete, but it keeps me moving, which is the goal.

The virtual walks also prepare me to participate in the 5K Canada Army Run, which I plan to do annually as long as I can. Although my participation is more of a walk/run/walk now, the entry fee and any related fundraising goes to Soldier On to support veterans overcoming physical and mental challenges.

No matter where we are in the cycle of life, we have a myriad of options available to us to do what we enjoy, and we should grab the one that appeals to us the most. I like to think of it as surfing life by latching onto a metaphorical wave and riding it until you're satisfied, and then, finding another one. Once we accept the fact we only go around once, it's time to make the most of it, even if that's when we retire.

CHAPTER EIGHTEEN

INSPIRATION VERSUS PERSPIRATION

There are many quotes floating around the internet about the time we should spend being inspired versus the time we should dedicate to hard work. Some refer to the ratio of one percent inspiration and ninety-nine percent perspiration while others are a little more extravagant on the inspiration side setting the ratio at 2:98. Still others have different interpretations.

The ratio doesn't matter. You get the picture. The biggest part of meeting a challenge is hard work, but sometimes we need inspiration to encourage us to keep working. Sometimes, we need inspiration as a reminder to perspire.

Before moving on to the perspiration part, let's look at how people are inspired. You'll recall Gabriella Varga's journey through an awful marriage and her struggles with obesity to find her niche as a competitive bodybuilder.

SOMETIMES WE NEED INSPIRATION AS A REMINDER TO PERSPIRE.

Evelyn and I experienced her transformation firsthand, and we were amazed, and yes, inspired by her dedication. But did all her hard work inspire her family? Let's hear from her two daughters, Paige and Kiera, as they share their thoughts about their mother.

First, Paige describes her mother's inspiration:

My mother and I are incredibly close. I owe a lot of my success to her, not only for the help and love she has given me through my life but also for all the valuable skills she's taught me. My mother is an extremely hard worker. Even during the most challenging times of her life, she always pulled through with a smile for my sister and me.

As I grew up and learned more about her life and the challenges she's faced, I gained more respect for her. She always used to tell me I was her number one cheerleader during her weight loss journey, going back to school to finish her degree, and then her masters in health quality. At the start, I began going to the gym with my mom to spend more time with her because everything she had going on limited her time. However, like her, I've always been athletic and enjoyed fitness. My mother taught me a lot about muscle overload and ways to eat clean. Eventually, I fell in love with fitness and how it makes me feel. So, in the fall of 2021, after my mom's first show. I decided I also wanted to compete.

She became my coach. During my first prep, my mom was highly supportive, and I can honestly say I probably would have never been able to do it without her encouragement. In the fall of 2022, I did my first show, which allowed me to understand finally the hype of wanting to compete. My mother taught me you could do it all if you truly put your mind to it. She's a full-time nurse, owns her own business in healthcare, is a bodybuilder, and is working on her masters at Queen's University in Kingston, Ontario while also being a wife and mother to two daughters. Because of her willingness to aspire to achieve her goals, she set an example that will impact me for the rest of my life. I will forever be grateful and extremely lucky to have such a fantastic parent.

Kiera describes her mother like this:

My mother is the most important person in my life, she's been there for me since day one, and I wish I could have done the same for her when she needed it. I never knew what she went through with her marriage. She tried to keep it from me for as long as possible because she knew it would only hurt me. I learned a few years ago why she left my father. He wasn't a kind man, and he almost ruined her. It must have been terrifying to leave, but she knew she had to protect herself and her children. I remember she would tell us she was working the night shift at the hospital and that she'd be here to wake us up in the morning, take us to school, and be there when we got home. Now thinking about it, she must've been exhausted, but she was amazing. She is the most inspiring person I've ever met.

Not only did she raise two daughters alone, but she worked full-time to support us while encouraging us to spend time with our father because she knew we needed him in our lives. We have little in common as she likes fitness and I like… not fitness, but as much as we don't talk about her bodybuilding, I would always be in the kitchen helping her prep. It was our time, and I loved it. I aspire to be like her, to be that strong, to be that brave, to be that caring. She makes me want to do well, and I want to make her proud. She's my reason for trying, she's my strength and my weakness, my hope, and my best friend. I wouldn't have been able to do anything I have without her being there by my side, and I am so grateful for what she's done for me, I needed someone, and she was there, and now I hope she can come to me when she needs the same.

Gabriella and the rest of the group are inspirational, but they all had people who worked hard and inspired them. It's mutually beneficial. Gabriella inspired her family, and they inspired her. Dan Crépault and Brian Singh were both inspired by others to change their lives. They received initial support from family and friends, and once they arrived at the treatment center, others just like them inspired them. But that was only the beginning. Once they had the inspiration, the next step—and the biggest one—was the hard work to make it happen.

The farm where our parents raised my brothers and me is near a small town on the Canadian prairies. The dependence on events out of our control like the weather and the whims of the government setting quotas made farming too unstable as a career for me. But I wouldn't have wanted to grow up anywhere else. It's hard work, but I remember the good times on the farm, and there were many. There is nowhere that can assault the senses more than the farm. The wide-open spaces, the sights, sounds, and smells.... To this day, I love going back to visit relatives and for a reset or a reminder of what it's like. I enjoy seeing the multi-colored crops waving in the breeze, the dust wafting behind the heavy equipment working the fields, and the unobstructed views in any direction. There is the scent of clean air and wet earth after a nighttime rain, the sweet smell of freshly cut hay, and the sound of cows mooing and horses whinnying. I love the farm; I just wasn't made to be a farmer.

Farmers are an inspiration, working as hard as they do with little appreciation or financial reward. My parents were an inspiration to me. They weren't the most outgoing people, but their words had an impact. My story on the farm doesn't differ from any other young boy or girl raised in that environment. One quickly learns the meaning of hard work. I was hauling grain in a one-ton truck as soon as I could reach the pedals and helping on the farm as much as I could. If my brothers read this, they may dispute whether I helped as much as I think I did.

Even though I left the farm at eighteen, I will be forever grateful for being raised there. I honestly didn't know what I was going to do as I approached the end of my school years. Fortunately, the same aunt who took me through the Canadian Rockies when I was twelve showed me two newspaper ads for Chartered Accountancy students (now referred to in Canada as Chartered Professional Accountants). Like Karen, I didn't know what a Chartered Accountant was, but two things appealed to me about the ads. The first, was that the jobs were in Winnipeg, about 150 miles from the farm. The second was that students worked for the accounting firm for a salary while studying nights and weekends. In those days, the C.A. program required working at the firm and studying for five years, successfully completing eighteen subjects before writing four final examinations. A university degree was not a prerequisite then.

The success rate to complete the program wasn't high. We studied accounting, auditing, law, economics, computer programming, etc. It wasn't easy, and there were many nights I had to study after working all day while my friends were having fun. Evelyn and I married in 1970, and she also sacrificed, so that I could study. There were many times I thought of quitting, but two things inspired me to keep climbing.

The first was the common theme around the house growing up that if something is possible for someone, it was possible for us, too. We came to learn that wasn't entirely realistic, of course, but the message was that we should shoot for the moon. The second inspirational lesson was that good things only come through hard work. Our parents sacrificed to keep the farm operational during the lean years. Our dad kept going, even when hail wiped out the crops. It couldn't have been easy for our parents, and it was a reminder to me not to quit. I forged on, and it turned out to be one of the best decisions of my life. I followed up the C.A. designation with another three years of studying to obtain my Registered Industrial Accountant designation. Now, the governing bodies have combined the two designations into one.

As I look back on my career, I have to say it turned out well. I enjoyed my work in various federal government departments as an employee and consultant. I'm satisfied that I contributed and made good friends along the way. During that time, I took part on various volunteer boards and spent six years with Toastmasters International, finishing as District Governor with a Distinguished Toastmaster designation. More perspiration! I'm convinced my parents' parents inspired them to work hard, and they handed the work ethic down to my brothers and me. My wife and I have tried to pass it on to our kids, and I think I can proudly say mission accomplished. Trevor is a musician earning a living in Nashville and touring. He was gigging in clubs at fifteen. He has followed his passion and succeeded. Like any entrepreneur, during the pandemic when the entertainment business dried up, he had to work even harder and be resilient and flexible by switching to online shows and audiobook narration.

Chris is passing his work ethic along to his three children as the oldest has a job at fifteen. None of this happens without hard work, and I hope there is never a break in the cycle of passing along the work ethic from generation to generation.

Just because I retired from consulting didn't mean my life was over or that there would be no more perspiring. New doors opened, and I happily walked through. I grabbed the wave that came along and rode it until I was satisfied... then reached for the next. The hard work never stops. It just gets more satisfying.

CHAPTER NINETEEN

WORDS MATTER

Edwin explained how a change to the tenets of the Constitution altered Cameroon's path, resulting in the conflict endured by him and his family and thousands of others. Elisa recalled her friend encouraging her to publish her writings. Words matter!

After we completed our Kilimanjaro climb, we traveled by airplane to the town of Mwanza on the southern shores of Lake Victoria in northwest Tanzania. When Chris and I decided to climb, we resolved to use the mountain as a platform to raise money for the kids of Tanzania. We contacted five child-centered non-profit organizations to inform them of our plans and to offer to raise money for one of their projects. One responded. That one was Plan International Canada.

Plan International Canada is a member of a global organization that's dedicated to advancing children's rights and equality for girls. They quickly proposed a project that clicked with us. The project was to fund the building of a classroom at a primary school in Mwanza, about a two-hour flight from Moshi where the base of Mount Kilimanjaro is located. We decided we would write every donor's name on a Canadian flag that, hopefully, we would carry to Kilimanjaro's peak. The plan was to deliver it to the primary school after the climb.

We had no idea how much money we could raise, so we aimed for $5,000 and quickly surpassed that. We raised the goal to $8,000 and shot past that, too. Plan International Canada added another project to drill a borehole (well) at a preschool in Mwanza. By the time we left for Tanzania, we had covered the flag with over 200 names. Friends, relatives, and people we didn't know had contributed over $15,000! The flag inspired us to keep climbing, but it also put pressure on us. We desperately wanted to get the flag to the top for the people who had donated to our cause. I even dreamt one night on the mountain that the flag slipped out of our fingers and sailed away on the wind, never to be seen again.

We met with representatives of Plan International Tanzania in Mwanza, who drove us along paved streets past a variety of dilapidated houses, apartment buildings, churches, mosques, and fish processing plants. Large hills strewn with boulders surrounded the city. Builders had nestled houses among the rocks, and stone-covered islands rose from the waters of Lake Victoria. Appropriately, the locals refer to Mwanza as "Rock City."

Eventually, we arrived at a hard clay schoolyard. One tin-roofed concrete building, white on top and blue on the bottom, sat in the yard. The building housed two classrooms, where teachers educated hundreds of kids in shifts. Small, wide-eyed, curious smiling faces stared through the open windows. A group of teachers in brightly colored dresses and official looking dignitaries in dress shirts and pants greeted us at the primary school. The sun beat down on the hard clay, and thankfully, the teachers invited us to sit at shaded desks on a concrete veranda at the front of one of the school buildings. A gentleman translated the words of the teachers and dignitaries for us. They were polite and generous with their time but, I thought, a little withdrawn. The reason would soon become clear.

We presented the flag and soccer balls that we had brought with us. The head teacher's eyes welled up at the sight of the soccer balls. It was another moment we'll never forget, but there was more to come. We got down to the business of the work we had done to raise money. One teacher said something to us I'll never forget. She said, "Often, the *Mzungu* (translates from Swahili to white person) make promises and don't deliver." Admittedly, it took me aback a bit. After all, we took the time and put in the effort to raise money to help build a classroom for them. But upon reflection, I understand the comment. It's easy to make promises when we're caught up in the moment. On the plane ride home, the realization could easily set in that there isn't the time or wherewithal to do as promised. The hard part is delivering.

The lesson I took from this is that words matter. People who promised to do something but failed to deliver had obviously disappointed the teachers. The reasons may have been perfectly valid, but we need to be careful what we say and to whom. From my perspective, I took her words as a challenge. Maybe that's what she intended. If so, her strategy worked because her words became inspirational for me.

We came home, and Evelyn and I continued to fundraise. Over the next ten years with the help and amazing support of good friends, we held golf tournaments, variety shows, cocktail parties, and events for kids to raise money to complete the funding for the classroom and borehole. We continued over the ten years to contribute funds to a sanitation project to provide latrines and washing facilities at schools and a micro finance project to help young women start small businesses. We also raised money for a Wounded Warriors Canada project to train elite service dogs to operate with veterans suffering from post-traumatic stress disorder.

I can't describe the satisfaction of helping others. Each time we did it, it became more inspirational, and it encouraged us to just keep climbing. Evelyn and I went back to Africa in 2011 to see the results of our projects to that date. The same people treated us like royalty this time. The kids were still smiling, but more importantly, the attitude of the teachers and dignitaries had changed completely. Everyone was friendly and outgoing and not the least bit withdrawn. With our funds and amounts raised by others, the schoolyard now held six classrooms instead of two.

There are also instances where the communication is silent, but the insight and inspiration are just as powerful. Evelyn and I attended a meeting in Dar es Salaam, Tanzania, where women either borrowed or paid back seed money to start small business. The organizers conducted the meeting until one woman, short in stature but tall with pride, paid back the money she had borrowed. A red coverup draped around her shoulders and a scarf covered her head. She didn't look in our direction, but when we asked what she did, she shyly responded to the translator without making eye contact. We were told she walked to a market to buy fish, returned home, cooked it, and resold it for a small profit. We said, "Congratulations," and her face broadened like a beam of sunlight that lit the room. The pride she felt for being able to pay back the money she borrowed and contribute to her family's well-being was palpable. She didn't have to say a word. Her expression told her story.

Our inspiration was the words of the teacher that day on the porch in Mwanza, Tanzania and the face of the woman paying back her money in Dar es Salaam. Listening and observing pays enormous dividends. A good friend's wise mother once told her, "You don't learn while you're talking."

Humans are social creatures by nature, so we love to communicate. The avenues for communication have blown wide open with texting, emails, social media, and phone calls, although the latter is becoming less and less common. But it's only communication if it works both ways. Whether it's at meetings or in one-on-one conversation, there's always the person who just has to be heard. Good things can happen when we just shut up for a minute or two. The person who doesn't listen is shortchanging themselves. Communication is a two-way street, and by not listening, we are missing the opportunity to hear another opinion and learn something.

I'm glad I come from a family of listeners. My mother, especially, talked little. However, when she did, everybody listened. Our parents didn't need to raise their voices. One withering look was enough. I think because of that, I listened to what the teacher in Tanzania said. Even though we had raised enough for the classroom and borehole, her words tugged at my heart strings, and it inspired me to come home and do more. The satisfaction from our fundraising was enormous.

Dan Crépault and Brian Singh listened when it really mattered... before it was too late. Sometimes, it takes a while to realize that someone else has something important to say. Something worthwhile to listen to. They listened to the counselors and colleagues at the treatment center, and it saved them. It allowed them to reverse the downward spiral they were in and to climb toward reclaiming their lives.

Time has made me even more acutely aware of how words matter. A former colleague recently told me, "I've never forgotten when you said..." I didn't recall saying it, but it seemed to have had a positive impact on him. It has happened more than once. I'm sure we can all remember someone from years ago whose words impacted us. It's just a reminder that what we say lingers in the minds of others, so we need to be positive with our statements and careful with what we say. Sadly, the discourse has become more negative since the pandemic, but we can all do our bit to turn that negativity around.

I posted, "Every mountain top is within reach if you just keep climbing," on my blog, and things developed quickly. A woman sent me a message asking if she could tattoo an excerpt from it on her arm for inspiration. "Of course," I said, but I couldn't imagine it having such an impact. Requests came in to use it on a stamp for scrapbooking, t-shirts, posters, coffee mugs, and most recently, to paint it on the wall of a café.

I came up with the motto as a reminder to myself to keep climbing, no matter the situation, but it has resonated with others.

Our words really do matter.

CHAPTER TWENTY

PEOPLE ARE PEOPLE

All the inspirational people in this book are different. They have different goals, different ideas, different ways of arriving at their destination. We're all different. But traveling the globe makes one thing abundantly clear. Whether we are in Africa, the Caribbean, the U.K., or anywhere else, we are more similar than we are different. People are people despite our differences.

Edwin and his family, stuck in the middle of a conflict in Cameroon, have the same hopes and aspirations as you and me. They just need the opportunities the war took away from them for the last several years.

When Evelyn and I traveled back to Tanzania in 2011, we wanted to satisfy ourselves that the money we had raised was going to the projects as intended. We visited the primary school and preschool where the classrooms and borehole were supposed to be. Instead of one blue and white concrete building housing two classrooms, three buildings and six classrooms occupied the space. The attitude of the children hadn't changed. They still smiled, despite the challenges they faced.

The teachers, happier that we delivered on our promise, greeted us with smiles and led us into one of the new classrooms where they had hung our Canadian flag beside the Tanzanian flag. They also pointed out a handwritten sign in English thanking us for the work we did to provide the new classroom. The kids danced in a choreographed show for us, and they helped us plant trees in the schoolyard. Every one of the approximately 400 kids wanted to high-five us. We felt like royalty, but when we thought about it, we realized we had done one simple thing. We kept a promise, which gave them hope.

A lack of reputable rigs in the area meant the borehole we funded with donations received had yet to be completed, but we later received photos confirming that the drilling team finished the work. The borehole eventually provided clean water to 13,000 people in the community.

After seeing the spot at the preschool in 2011 where the borehole would be, Plan International Tanzania drove us to a dormitory for young schoolgirls that was under construction. This time, a new group of dignitaries and teachers awaited us along with about 900 schoolkids, at least half of whom were girls. We learned that some girls walked up to ten miles for water and returned home in the dark, leaving them vulnerable. Everything possible was being done to correct that situation.

The dormitory under construction would eventually house one hundred of the most vulnerable girls. After the speeches concluded, Plan International Tanzania invited us to tour the construction. Three girls took the Plan International Canada representative, while three others guided Evelyn, and three guided me. When we completed the tour, one said to me, "So, when are you taking me to Canada?" It was a sweet question until I considered the consequences. She was completely serious. She was an orphan, so she had nothing to keep her there. She saw it as an opportunity, and she was determined to find something better. I'm convinced that if I had driven up to the gate in a car at midnight, she would have jumped in, likely accompanied by a few friends. Who knows what would have happened if they left with the wrong people?

The girls have hopes and dreams just like we do, but the prospect of being unable to reach their dreams rested in the back of their minds. When we spoke to the girls as a group, two wanted to be pilots, two aspired to be doctors, two had their hopes set on becoming lawyers, and one a nurse. Their hopes and dreams do not differ from those of our kids. Sadly, the challenges faced by our children multiply for the kids living in an undeveloped country. But they keep dreaming and keep climbing.

We all receive the annoying phone calls and emails originating in Nigeria, India, and other countries, advising us we are the long-lost descendant of someone, and if we click on the link, we will start the process to receive an inheritance of millions of dollars. They are scams and there are hundreds of variations of the same thing. Lately, I've been receiving two or three requests weekly to connect on LinkedIn with young men and women in Nigeria purporting to be book marketing experts.

The messages are irritating, but let's put ourselves in their shoes for a moment. They are doing their best to earn a living. Actual jobs are unavailable. I'm not condoning what they're doing because they're trying to take advantage of people who may not know any better. As the saying goes, desperate times call for desperate measures, and I think that's what's going on. A friend in Tanzania told me about a woman he knows who is doing the bookkeeping and other jobs for a bar eight hours a day, six days a week for $15 a month! While the cost of living is less than in the developed world, it's still high. Yet they keep climbing and doing the best they can with what they have.

We learned through our travels that there is tremendous power in the indomitable human spirit to overcome immense hardship. Those of us fortunate enough to be born in a developed nation can only imagine what their challenges must be like. When we visited Tanzania, it occurred to me how valuable it would be if every student in the western world could visit an impoverished nation for a few days. It's tremendously enriching to experience the thoughts and living conditions of others. The educational value of travel is immeasurable.

We've also been fortunate to examine our surroundings through the lens of friends who are new Canadians. They view everything as new and exciting, and sometimes, challenging. Things that we take for granted are different for them. Of course, it would be the same if the roles were reversed. Experiencing our country through their eyes returns many times over whatever help we might be able to give them. It has been an enriching experience.

Karen wrote of the delightful South Koreans she met during her Atacama run. Her initial reservations turned into an enriching experience as she became more familiar with them.

We hope we changed the lives of a few people in Africa with a little effort and the combined contributions of many friends and acquaintances. Maybe we made some young people feel important, that someone cares. Perhaps, some lifted themselves out of the cycle of poverty with the help of the small business loans. Maybe we helped to make some dreams come true by funding the borehole, so the girls who normally fetched water could go to school. We'll never know for sure. We hope so.

All anyone needs is a chance and a purpose.

Of course, we have similar issues scattered throughout North America, but not as widespread, and we have the means to deal with them. Sometimes, what we are lacking is the will. It doesn't matter where we are in the world, people are the same. The general population doesn't sew distrust among nations. People just want to feel that they are contributing to society and that they can support their families. It's that desire that keeps people climbing. People are all created equally no matter how different we appear to be. We all have a right to respect, dignity, and purpose.

CHAPTER TWENTY-ONE

COMMUNITY

As we have seen from the stories told by our inspirational group, support is essential to getting us through the many challenges we face. Whether the challenges are hill-like or mountain-size, we often can't conquer them by ourselves. Obviously, family is important, but sometimes, for whatever reason, it's not enough. We need to do a little self-assessment to determine the type of support we need.

Elisa had an on-again, off-again relationship with religion. But before the surgery which threatened her ability to play her beloved fiddle, she rushed to the church for one last opportunity to play. Now, she has rediscovered religion, and family and friends surround her. Probably, she doesn't know most of the thousands of friends she has accumulated on social media, but like all of us, they are part of a very important community in her life.

Karla and Karen both relied on the community of the Running Room to get started on their journeys. Dan and

Brian needed the community at the treatment center that they credit for seeing them through. Edwin relied on his family as much as they relied on him through the worst of the conflict in Cameroon. Jen Gilroy credits her parents, grandparents, and caring teachers and librarians for helping her through her youth. Today, she's appreciative of her husband, daughter, extended family and friends, readers, and a strong writing community for supporting her in life and writing. Gabriella relied on her coach to get her started on the path toward a lifetime of fitness.

Before I even asked Chris if he would be interested in climbing Kilimanjaro, I sought assurance from others that the climb would be doable. They represented my first layer of support. By contacting several people who climbed Kilimanjaro, I satisfied myself it could be done with the right preparation, even though some of the initial comments didn't sound that encouraging. One said, "I don't think I should tell you how I felt." Another said, "You do not want to use the park toilets when one hundred percent of the people have diarrhea." For the record, I did not find that to be the case. I can't comment on the park toilets since our porters carried our portable apparatus, but thankfully, the one hundred percent number was an exaggeration.

The comments from the community of climbers I approached gave me enough confidence to proceed. I still needed to know that Evelyn would be comfortable with me going. Without that, I wouldn't have been able to do it. I also asked my brother, Keith, who lay very sick in a hospital bed. I didn't know what to expect when we returned. They gave me the final encouragement I needed.

I realized how important community is in our lives when we moved from a suburb in the east end to one in the southwest part of the city in 2004. It wasn't like we moved to a different part of the country. It's a thirty-minute drive, but the friends who would drop over for a beer or to help with some project around the house or yard wouldn't be doing that anymore. We couldn't just wander down the street and do the same. Even though the distance was not far, things that we took for granted weren't there anymore.

We still see our friends from the east end, of course, but it's more like every month or two rather than every few days. Our son and grandkids lived in the new area, but that was the extent of the people we knew at the time we moved. Evelyn decided one day after the move that she was going to church, and I tagged along. It turned out to be significant decision. Not only did we get the spiritual renewal we needed, but it also provided the opportunity to meet new friends and gave us a community to belong to.

The value of community became obvious to us in the summer of 2021 when an intense windstorm called a derecho hit our city. People in the area lost power for various lengths of time. We lost power in our house for five and a half days. As people, we always need support but no more than at a time like that. People have suffered through much worse than we did and would attest to what you're about to read on a much larger scale, but we saw our version of the strength of community firsthand.

We contacted long-time friends and those we had known a shorter time through church who still had electricity. Some shared space in their freezers for our frozen food. Others brought coffee or invited us to their place to charge our devices. Another lent us a portable device to charge our phones. Our neighbor in the same predicament as us, purchased a generator about midway through the week and let us plug in our water heater and freezer. People called to check on us. One person filled a cooler full of snow and ice from the scrapings off a local hockey rink's ice surface to help keep the remaining food in the house cold. As I write this, these all seem like first world problems, but we considered ourselves extremely fortunate to have the support of our community of friends and neighbors to help us through a difficult situation.

A similar example of community support occurred in 2000. We owned a six-unit apartment building west of the city. On December 20th, we received a shocking phone call advising us that our fully rented building was on fire. By the time we arrived at the site, the firefighters stood by their trucks drinking coffee. The building was beyond saving. Fortunately, all the renters escaped, but the fire left them homeless. The community stepped up in a huge way, gathering money, a mountain of clothing for everyone, and toys for the kids.

These stories are not unique. Every time we hear of a disaster of any kind, stories surface about the generosity of people. But just as important as the material things people contribute, is the moral support they provide. Everyone needs that as evidenced by our own experience and the inspirational stories in the preceding chapters. In my experience, social support contributes to physical and mental well-being, whether we need someone to lean on during a crisis or just to talk to occasionally. The support we provide others can be as simple as listening, encouraging, or providing praise or constructive feedback. We all need it from time to time, and we're all capable of offering it when needed.

DEFINING
SUCCESS

CHAPTER TWENTY-TWO

CHALLENGES GIVE US EXPERIENCE

It's apparent now that life's path resembles the road from Kahului to the town of Hana in east Maui, Hawaii with its 620 curves and forty-nine one-way bridges over an 84-kilometer (52-mile) distance. The challenges, big and small, pile up. We can overcome most of them easily, but some are more difficult. Each of the people in this book either gave themselves challenges or had challenges thrown at them they didn't want. The common denominator is that they either overcame their challenges or are doing their best to deal with them. Each challenge they faced prepared them for the next one.

We deal with challenges from the time we are old enough to recognize them. I don't know that challenges become less frequent as we age, but for most, they do become different. The challenge of the career path to follow comes and goes. Same for the challenge of finding a life partner and starting a family. As we move into our retirement years, the challenges turn to health issues and watching friends and colleagues pass on. Bereavement presents an enormous challenge that is difficult to overcome. Lately, there have been announcements every second day, it seems, about entertainment icons we idolized in our youth passing away. A new challenge arises, that of staring down our own mortality.

Facing challenges is easier for some than others. We've all heard that so-and-so is good at everything they do. A different way of looking at it, is that people are more likely to gravitate to things they are good at, giving the illusion they are good at everything. If a person realizes they can't sing after warbling in the shower, it's unlikely they'll volunteer to be the lead singer in a band. Or at least, maybe they shouldn't. Admittedly, some are so passionate about a particular thing they will do it anyway, whether or not they are good. They are challenging themselves and have set their own measure of success. Just taking part is a success if it's something we feel strongly enough about. The bonus is that each one prepares us for the next one.

Whether we realize it, life would be pretty boring without challenges. Throughout my life, I've realized that if most people don't have enough challenges in their lives, they will create them. Some suggest that life begins when we start to feel uncomfortable. Things start to get exciting when we take on a challenge that is unfamiliar territory or completely foreign to us. I discovered that about myself when I accepted the challenge of improving my fitness level. Of course, to ignore the doctor's advice could have meant I wouldn't be around today, so I had a rather large incentive. Once that was done, Chris and I challenged ourselves to climb the mountain and raise money for the kids in Tanzania. One of my biggest challenges arose even before that. Like many people, I was completely uncomfortable speaking in public. I joined Toastmasters International for six years. I got to where I enjoyed speaking in public (depending on the topic), although the butterflies never go away entirely. Toastmasters teaches that we just need to organize the butterflies so that they fly in formation. It would prove invaluable throughout my career and into my retirement years and led to the presentations we made on our climb and fundraising.

Offramps have been available for most of my challenges, but when they involve settling for something less, it's disappointing. I'm not about to take an offramp unless I gave the challenge my best. I mentally establish a threshold of success that will satisfy me.

I learned that challenges give us experiences that shape who we are. Challenges are like building blocks. Each one we experience strengthens us. We learn how to deal with them better each time a new one comes up. When faced with a challenge, the experience of putting one foot in front of the other on the mountain gives me the strength to do pretty much everything I set my mind to, or at least to try. In short, I learned how to just keep climbing.

There are pages on the internet and books filled with useful advice on dealing with challenges. It's mostly common sense. First, we need to define the nature of the challenge. If we don't know exactly what the challenge is, or if we need help to deal with it, we should seek a professional, a friend, or a community to help. Remaining positive and setting realistic goals in the face of a challenge is critical to successfully defeating it.

CHALLENGES ARE LIKE BUILDING BLOCKS. EACH ONE WE EXPERIENCE STRENGTHENS US.

If you will bear with me, I'll apply my health situation to these suggestions. My challenge was my elevated triglycerides and the threat of a heart attack or stroke. I had to do something about it. I sought help through a personal trainer, and family and friends would hike with me to keep me motivated. Even though I sometimes didn't feel like it, I forced myself to meet with my trainer or go hiking on a Sunday morning. My measure of success was the follow-up medical test that assured me the triglycerides were back in the range they should be, which I eventually met and then some.

That was the experience, the building block, if you will, that led to climbing Kilimanjaro and fundraising, which then led to writing nine books and counting. Each provided valuable experience that shaped who I am today. Preceding that, the challenge of obtaining a Chartered Professional Accountant designation led to my career. We walk through doors and accept challenges we meet on the other side, and each provides experience that readies us for the next challenge.

CHAPTER TWENTY-THREE

THE COMMON THREADS

An adjective is applied to each inspiring person at the beginning of their respective chapters describing the quality that I think makes them do what they do. Jen Gilroy demonstrated courage by making a big career change to follow her passion and become a writer. Gabriella Varga overcame a myriad of challenges to become a champion bodybuilder, revealing tremendous resilience. Karla Del Grande and Karen Meades exhibited determination and tenacity, respectively, with their running. Dan Crépault and Brian Singh reclaimed their lives by fighting off the demons of drug abuse to become exemplary citizens of society. Elisa Magagna remains positive despite the adversity she faces, and Edwin and his family continue to be resolute and unswerving in their desire to remain in their town in the face of armed conflict.

But when I stopped to think about it, the descriptors are interchangeable. Jen Gilroy is determined. Elisa Magagna is courageous. Gabriella reclaimed her life. Dan and Brian remained positive despite their setbacks. Edwin and his family are resilient. Karla is tenacious, and Karen is resolute. Change them up any way you want. There is a commonality among all of them that makes them who they are.

Earlier in the book, we examined why people challenge themselves when they don't really have to. Life is full of challenges so why add to it? The answers are in the lessons we learn as we keep climbing to overcome any challenge, and each one gives us experience to face the next. In my case, the lessons learned came down to the five Ps: persistence, patience, preservation, perspective, and pride. I'm sure I can say the same for each of the eight people who accomplished their extraordinary challenges or who are facing adversity.

The mission becomes personal for those who give themselves challenges, which some might consider a little selfish. Loved ones take extreme measures to provide support. When I trained to climb Kilimanjaro, Evelyn and I would drive to a trailhead somewhere, and she would read a book for an hour while I hiked. Then she waited and worried while Chris and I were away chasing our dream. Writing can be another selfish endeavor as countless hours are spent alone with a computer. Each of the inspiring people who challenged themselves referred to sacrifices made by their families while they followed their passion or turned their lives around. One or a combination of all the qualities already mentioned drove them to overcome their challenges, but on the surface, it involved a cost to loved ones, at least temporarily.

We need to examine this so-called selfishness closer. Each of us who took on a personal challenge did so to become a better version of ourselves. We did it for the satisfaction of knowing we *could* do it. Accomplishing the challenge makes us better people, and as pointed out in the previous chapter, lays the groundwork for the next challenge. The next challenge could be much bigger than something for personal satisfaction.

It's worthwhile re-examining the impact of the challenge that each undertook. By changing her career, and with her husband's support, Jen spent more time as a caregiver for her family and could focus on her writing. Her books are gifts to her readers and will be available forever for people to discover and enjoy. Gabriella is a huge inspiration to her family and is giving back by educating women on the value of nutrition and health. Karla shows other women there are no limits to what they can do, no matter the age, and trains at a facility for children and adults of all abilities. Karen just keeps climbing through teaching, various volunteer activities, and motivational presentations.

Dan is now the program director at Harvest House, and Brian is a staff member. Both have rediscovered family and want to inspire others just like them. Elisa wants to tell her story and be an inspiration to people facing the same situation she is in, and Edwin also wants to show people that, if he and his family can overcome the adversity they are facing, anyone can do the same.

Our respective journeys may have started out for self-improvement and to overcome personal challenges, but not one of them ended that way. Each of us became inspired to take action to help others. Although we may not realize it at the time, that becomes the real satisfaction when we just keep climbing.

We all have the qualities to pursue our dreams, overcome a challenge, or fight adversity. It depends how badly we want it. And when we do, we all want to pay it forward.

CHAPTER TWENTY-FOUR

WHAT IS SUCCESS?

Most of us wake up in the morning with choices. We can either choose to be happy or get our day off to a poor start by getting up grumpy. Granted, some just need that first cup of coffee to be in a better mood. The choice we make each morning has a great deal to do with how the rest of our day will go and might determine our success.

After hearing the stories people shared with me, I was curious to know how each defined success. Success is different for all of us, and I believe our definition changes with age and experience. Things that may be important to us when we are young, no longer seem that relevant as we wander through life. Our priorities change and, therefore, so does our definition of success. My dream as a teenager of having a mansion, yacht, and several luxury cars soon became overly optimistic, but I still consider my life to have been successful, even without the shiny accessories.

Each of the people who told me their stories has a different definition of what success means to them. Each inspires us in different ways, and each story has been driven by life's path. They willingly shared their definition of success at this point in their lives. I also asked our sons how they would define success. Anyone involved in the arts knows how difficult it can be to make a successful career out of following a passion. This is how Trevor defines success:

> *Being in the music business, I used to believe that fame, and wealth defined success—record contracts, music videos, awards, a stay or two at the Betty Ford Clinic, etc. I was all ambition and drive and forever facing forward. Now, armed with age and experience, I've also been given the gift of perspective, and I remember to look back and take stock occasionally and appreciate where I've been.*
>
> *Not to mention that somebody moved the musical goalposts—you don't need a record contract to make music—people can do it in their bedroom closets. Literally anybody can make a music video and post it to multiple platforms. Awards are nice, but you realize that's not the reason to do what you're doing.*
>
> *I watched as friends gained accolades and got closer to realizing their— and my—dreams which was another important lesson about improving my mindset. Their successes do not detract from mine and there's room for everybody.*
>
> *After a couple of years of struggling after moving to Nashville, I've been able to make my living doing nothing but music (and music related things). I played over 300 shows in one year. I've seen a lot of the world. I've met some cool and interesting people. My bills are paid. And best of all, I have a great home life where the situation is loving, healthy, and mutually supportive.*
>
> *To sum it up, success is equal parts ambition, attitude, and perspective—and if you can be a little philosophical, it doesn't hurt.*

Chris followed the entrepreneurial path for several years and now performs various accounting functions for an international firm. He defines success like this:

In my mind, to properly define success you need to break it down into different areas of your life. At work, it is the achievement of common goals as a team to further the success of your clients or your own business (ideally both). Success at home is maintaining a positive relationship with your kids and your significant other and having the freedom to take your vacation time and spend proper quality time with family. It is not always about dollars and cents; it can sometimes just be about having the ability to brighten a room with your humor or smile. Success is not a destination, but it's a journey of finding the little victories in everyday life by focusing not on what went wrong, but instead looking at what went right through the process.

Jen Gilroy had an established career but followed her passion. She defines success this way:

I define success by doing meaningful work, using my skills to the best of my ability, and continuing to learn and grow personally and professionally. Beyond work, success for me also means living a balanced life with time for family, friends, and hobbies.

As an author, it's having the sense of "making a difference" too and hearing from readers that my stories have touched and helped them at difficult points in their own lives.

Gabriella Varga overcame a hard life to compete on a bodybuilding stage with women ten years younger. She defines success:

You would think that the success in my story is losing 117 pounds or maybe winning first place, but when asked to define success, I really had to ponder the question. Success to me in the beginning was to win, to be number one, to be the fittest. Since, I have competed in three shows, placing in all. But the real win here is the dedication and work I put in for me. Since January 2021, I have consistently worked almost every day. When I was doing my prep in the beginning and people asked how I did it, I said, "It wasn't an option." Three years later, I'm still in the gym almost every day, and it's not a question now, it's my lifestyle. My day isn't complete if I don't work out, and I no longer feel guilt when I don't go to the gym but the opposite, I feel like I'm missing something. The success of my story was the consistency and the dedication I gave myself so that I could be a better version of me, for me and everyone else.

Karla Del Grande is still sprinting at age seventy and hoping to do so into her nineties. Here's how she defines success:

I see success as doing the best that I can, getting better and better in a season of racing, and achieving the goals that I have in mind. And enjoying it.

Karen Meades challenged herself way beyond anything most of us would ever imagine. If a challenge seems to be too big, we only need to read Karen's story to realize we can overcome whatever we are facing. Karen describes success:

I think of life as a story—I am creating the story—it is my story, and I try to imagine what that story will be. You know when you have that moment during the day when you are daydreaming, I visualize myself at an old age—maybe ninety years old in a rocking chair, telling my story to my grandchildren—and I think, 'I want it to be a story I am proud to share, an exciting story, one with intrigue, love, adventure, a kick-ass story!'

Most importantly, I don't want my story to be about a day-to-day routine. I know I have to do, say, laundry, but I would like to catch up on my laundry after a week of, say, running through the Amazon Jungle!

I think positive thoughts. I derive a positive sense of well-being from those thoughts. I want to be part of something, something with a purpose, something larger than me.

Success to me is when I can see that I set the goal, did the hard work, completed something, and said 'good job Karen' to myself. Another piece of the puzzle falls into place. It feels positive and constructive to acknowledge the effort. I wasn't the loser who didn't win, I was the winner who accomplished the goal within my skills and abilities.

Dan Crépault initially chose the wrong path but reclaimed his life with perseverance and hard work. This is how he defines success:

For me, success is about becoming a better version of myself, the version that God made me to be, and helping others to do the same. It's not about having more money so much as being more content and enjoying my life more. There are things I aspire to achieve that would make me feel more successful too, like writing fiction or helping Harvest House continue for another forty years. At this stage in my life, fatherhood is another major determinant of success. If I can break the cycles of addiction, anger, anxiety, etc., in myself, so that my son does not inherit them from me, I will consider that to be an important success.

Brian Singh made similar choices to Dan, and he also found his way back. He defines success this way:

> *For me, my success has been overcoming an extremely difficult part of my life that could have most likely killed me, picking myself out of the gutter, and using my experiences as a positive to help others that are in the same situation that I was. Achieving the vision that I saw for myself when I was lying in that hospital bed. Success to me would mean helping to save lives with my story and experiences—even if it is just one life. Success to me is sitting here today, with almost two years of sobriety, and looking forward to another fifty. Success to me is now being a staff member at the very drug treatment center that I went to and now working to become an addictions counsellor. Success to me is a continued journey that will not stop until the day I die.*

Elisa Beth Magagna faces her mortality with a charm, grace, and strength that would be impossible to achieve for most of us in a similar situation, but her attitude should be a lesson to all of us who are facing a difficult time. Here is how Elisa defines success:

> *Success is simply making a positive difference for the people I love. I remember looking back on my son's death, and the first several years, all I could remember was the pain of taking him off life support and watching him die. But over a decade later, I couldn't fully remember the sadness or the heartache. I remembered a time when he held my finger, I remembered the love. That's when I realized the only thing strong enough to withstand the test of time isn't the pain or the tragedy of hardships... it's the love.*

The Cameroon conflict has placed Edwin and his family in an untenable position, but he handles his plight in a truly inspirational manner. His definition of success is short and to the point, understandable given the situation he and his family are in. Edwin said:

> *I don't want any child growing to have the same life I had. No family should go through what my family went through, I wish I could change the world.*

When I decided to write this book, I knew I wanted some inspirational stories for people to take away with them. Something very interesting happened. When I put a call out asking people to share their inspirational stories, no one responded. Yet, when I approached people that I knew had stories to tell, not one turned me down. They were all very forthcoming and honest with their stories, and I'm deeply appreciative.

I think there's a reason no one came forward initially. People are inherently humble and don't think their stories would be inspirational to anyone. When they're in the moment, they're just going through life doing what they want to—or must do. It's only when others point out that the stories are inspirational that the owner will come forward. Remember Elisa's friend telling her how much her story helped her? It was only then that she published her book.

Chris and I experienced the same thing. It was only when we started doing presentations, we realized there was interest in our story. I discovered people found my story of climbing the mountain at age sixty to be inspirational. Telling the story about the impact of money raised for the kids of Tanzania and the service dog program for Wounded Warriors encouraged people to contribute. We don't realize the impact we are having. We may do things for our own reasons sometimes, but if it turns out we inspire others, all the better.

Looking back now from 40,000 feet, I realize that our definition of success changes as we navigate the trials and tribulations of life. In my early years, I chased the big house and shiny cars. It was more about the trappings. But now, I realize success is having the love and support of family and friends and watching our kids and grandkids have their own successes, knowing that as parents, we have done our best to lay the groundwork.

I've been fortunate to win a few accolades for various accomplishments along the way, and it's nice when someone else perceives you've been successful at something. But I discovered the real measure is our own satisfaction with each accomplishment. The genuine reward is that warm feeling we get knowing we've done the best we can with any challenge handed to us or that we chose to undertake.

As I reflect on the stories of each of our inspirational people, I understand we can't use the success of others to measure our own. I will never body build like Gabriella, but I will go to the gym. Nor will I sprint like Karla, but I'll walk/run the Canada Army Run for as many years as I'm physically able. I will never run the Atacama like Karen, but I will continue to walk the Great Wall of China virtually, and when that is done, I plan to take on another walking challenge.

AT THE END OF THE DAY, THE COMPLETE BODY OF WORK, NOT INDIVIDUAL GAINS AND LOSSES, MEASURES SUCCESS.

I'm inspired by the tenacity and grit, the honesty and forthrightness, the perseverance, and dedication of each of the inspiring group. Most of all, it's the determination of each to reach their goals, no matter what they are. It's the will to just keep climbing.

Success is recognizing the five Ps that each challenge gives us to build on. It's having no regrets. It's catching every interesting, passing wave and riding it for all it's worth, no matter our age. It's continuing to live life to the fullest and going to bed at night with the feeling the day has been complete, and that hopefully, we have made it enjoyable for someone else through our words or actions. It's accepting that we are all people, despite our differences.

In my mind, success is understanding that life isn't a sprint. It's a long obstacle course. It's understanding that we are going to make mistakes along the way, giving ourselves consent to do so, and learning from them. At the end of the day, the complete body of work, not individual gains and losses, measures success.

There are millions of similar inspirational stories out there. We're surrounded by them. We just need to take notice. I didn't want to include too many in this book because I thought it would detract from the power of the stories people so generously shared. I hope the stories achieve their purpose by inspiring you to reach for greater heights, make a choice to reverse paths, or meet adversity head on, no matter how dire the situation. I hope you will pick up the stories and read them over and over, especially any time you need a little inspiration.

And remember, every mountain top is within reach if you just keep climbing.

EPILOGUE

CHAPTER TWENTY-FIVE

WHAT'S ANOTHER MOUNTAIN?

Since writing the stories of these eight amazing people, life has dropped more mountains to climb in front of two of them. As one would anticipate from the spirit and attitude displayed throughout their stories, they both absolutely refuse to stop climbing. To them, it's just another mountain to conquer.

Doctors told Elisa Magagna she had terminal melanoma and two years to live in 2020. She stayed positive throughout the treatments, always taking the time to look her best and setting and reaching new goals. She is upfront about her condition with family and friends and continually encourages people in similar situations. Unfortunately, she received news recently that another tumor had been discovered in her brain, which would lead to another round of radiation.

Obviously, there have been dark days for Elisa and her family since, but she deals with it in the best way she knows how. She just keeps climbing, remaining positive. She plays her violin. She reaches out to her followers on Facebook with videos, inspiring others facing similar challenges to stay strong. Lately, she has been posting humorous videos with her husband about worse things than terminal cancer. As each challenge surfaces in Elisa's life, she faces them and keeps fighting. Whenever we have dark days, we need look no further than Elisa for inspiration.

Karen Meades has also been dealt a new challenge since her story was written. Ultramarathon runners must produce a medical certificate proving they are fit before participating in a race. Karen has been under a cardiologist's care for years due to an enlarged heart, which the doctor attributed to her training. In fact, since little is known about the effect of intense physical training on the female body, Karen has been somewhat of a case study.

When the required testing was done prior to her run across the U.K., it produced a shocking result. The doctor started the conversation with, "How are you feeling?" Although perplexed, Karen responded that she felt fine. Despite some mild fatigue, which she attributed to her age, she had no other indication that something could be wrong. The doctor's second statement stunned her. "I'm really worried about your results." It turned out, Karen has cardiomyopathy, or scarring of the heart, which makes it harder for it to pump blood to the rest of the body. Other than the fatigue, the typical symptoms of shortness of breath, swelling of the legs, ankles, and feet, fluttering heart, etc., had not surfaced. However, the doctor told her that the run across the U.K. she had been training for was now out of the question. Worse yet, her running days are over.

Karen's condition is genetic and has nothing to do with her training. Despite the setback, she remains upbeat and positive. There had to be dark days for her too, with the news that her life had just changed in an instant… that she would no longer be able to do the thing she loved the most and excelled at. But she sees it as an opportunity to fit another puzzle piece into her pie of life. She says she loves walking and bird watching and will try yoga. And she cheers on her friends who continue to race the incredible distances in the harshest conditions that she has already conquered. I'm convinced Karen will find new satisfying challenges and conquer them as well. A metaphorical mountain popped up, she climbed over it, and she will keep going with as much determination and pride as she put into her racing.

Elisa and Karen continue to face their challenges with strength and single-mindedness. They each had a choice—to let the latest challenge overwhelm them or to face it, adjust, and continue to live their best life. The last thing either one wants, is for anyone to feel sorry for them. After the initial shock wore off, they are getting on with their lives in a way that is a lesson to us all.

Thank you for reading *Just Keep Climbing*.
If you like what you read, please consider leaving
a review at your favorite online book retailer.

ABOUT THE AUTHOR

Barry Finlay is the award-winning author of the inspirational travel adventure, *Kilimanjaro and Beyond – A Life-Changing Journey* (with his son Chris), the Amazon bestselling travel memoir, *I Guess We Missed the Boat* and five Amazon bestselling and award-winning thrillers comprising The Marcie Kane Thriller Collection: *The Vanishing Wife, A Perilous Question, Remote Access, Never So Alone,* and *The Burden of Darkness.* He has now released two books in his new mystery series, featuring retired reporter Jake Scott: *Searching For Truth* and *The Guardians of Truth.* Barry was featured in the 2012-13 Authors Show's edition of "50 Great Writers You Should Be Reading." He is a recipient of the Queen Elizabeth Diamond Jubilee medal for his fundraising efforts to help kids in Tanzania, Africa. Barry lives with his wife Evelyn in Ottawa, Canada.

Contact Barry Finlay

Author Website: www.barry-finlay.com

Facebook: https://www.facebook.com/AuthorBarryFinlay

Twitter: https://twitter.com/Karver2

Printed in the USA
CPSIA information can be obtained
at www.ICGtesting.com
LVHW040730051023
760204LV00003B/21

9 781777 139599